A Tourist in Africa

Books by Evelyn Waugh

PRB: An Essay on the Pre-Raphaelite Brotherhood (1926, 1982)
Rossetti: His Life and Works (1928)
Decline and Fall (1928)
Vile Bodies (1930)
Labels (1930)
Remote People (1931)
Black Mischief (1932)
A Handful of Dust (1934)
Ninety-Two Days (1934)
Edmund Campion (1935)
Mr Loveday's Little Outing and Other Sad Stories (1936)
Waugh in Abyssinia (1936)
Scoop (1938)
Robbery Under Law (1939)
Put Out More Flags (1942)
Work Suspended (1942)
Brideshead Revisited (1945)
When the Going was Good (1946)
Scott-King's Modern Europe (1947)
Wine in Peace and War (1947)
The Loved One (1948)
Work Suspended and Other Stories (1949)
Helena (1950)
The Holy Places (1952)
Men at Arms (1952)
Love Among the Ruins (1953)
Officers and Gentlemen (1955)
The Ordeal of Gilbert Pinfold (1957)
The Life of the Right Reverend Ronald Knox (1959)
A Tourist in Africa (1960)
Unconditional Surrender (1961)
Basil Seal Rides Again (1963)
A Little Learning (1964)
Essays, Articles and Reviews (1984)

A TOURIST IN AFRICA

Evelyn Waugh

METHUEN

First published in Great Britain 1960
by Chapman and Hall Ltd

This edition published 1985
by Methuen London Ltd
11 New Fetter Lane, London EC4P 4EE

© 1960 Evelyn Waugh

Printed in Great Britain
by Richard Clay (The Chaucer Press) Ltd
Bungay, Suffolk

British Library Cataloguing in Publication Data

Waugh, Evelyn
   A tourist in Africa.
   1. Africa, East—Description and travel—1951–
   I. Title
   916.76   DT426

ISBN 0-413-56960-8 (hardback)
ISBN 0-413-56980-2 (paperback)

1 · Departure

Childermas in England – Mrs Stitch in Genoa

28th December 1958.   On the third day after Christmas we commemorate the massacre of the Holy Innocents. Few candid fathers, I suppose, can regard that central figure of slate in Breughel's painting in Antwerp without being touched by sympathy. After the holly and sticky sweetmeats, cold steel.

I declare smugly that at 55 I am at the time of life when I have to winter abroad, but in truth I reached that age thirty years ago. Even when I thought I enjoyed fox-hunting my enthusiasm waned by Christmas. I have endured few English Februaries since I became self-supporting. February 1940 found me a probationary temporary second-lieutenant in an asbestos chalet on the English Channel; never again, I resolved. February 1941 was far from luxurious, but it was warm, in a densely crowded troopship steaming through the tropics on the great detour to Egypt; but in 1942 I was in a Nissen hut on a Scottish moor; never again. In those days the politicians had a lot to say about Freedom. They met – few will now recall – and guaranteed everyone Freedom from Fear. Did they also guarantee Freedom from

Religion? Something of the sort, I think. All I asked in that horrible camp was freedom to travel. That, I should like to claim, is what I fought for, but I did far too little actual fighting to make that boast effective.

Then when the war was over the politicians did what they could to keep us all wired in; but I escaped regularly. Nowadays, I suppose, if such things were still required, I could get a doctor to certify that I needed to go abroad for my health. I begin to stiffen early in December. Stooping, turning, kneeling, climbing in and out of modern motor-cars, which are constructed solely for contortionists, become increasingly painful. By Christmas I look out on the bare trees with something near melancholia.

Childermas is the Sabbat of *cafard*. I have just looked up this popular word in the dictionary and have learned, as no doubt the reader already knows, that its roots come from 'hypocrisy' and 'cant'. It is therefore peculiarly apt for the emotions with which the father of a family performs the jollities of Christmastide. It is at Childermas, as a rule, that I begin to make plans for my escape, for, oddly enough, this regularly recurrent fit of claustrophobia always takes me by surprise as, I am told, the pains of childbirth often surprise mothers. Writing now in high summer (for this is not the diary as I kept it. I am trying to make a book from the notes I took abroad), it seems hardly conceivable that I shall ever want to leave my agreeable house and family. But I *shall*, next Childermas, and no doubt I shall once more find myself with no plans made.

It is not so easy as it was thirty years ago to find a retreat. Tourism and politics have laid waste everywhere. Nor is 55 the best age for travel; too old for the jungle, too young for the beaches, one must seek refreshment in the spectacle of other people at work, leading lives quite different from one's own. There are few more fatiguing experiences than to mingle with the holiday-makers of the Jamaican North Shore, all older, fatter, richer, idler and more ugly than oneself. India is full of splendours that must be seen now or perhaps never, but can a man of 55 long endure a régime where wine is prohibited?

I have worked for eighteen months on the biography of a remarkable but rather low-spirited friend many years older than myself. I have read nothing and met no one except to further my work. Old letters, old dons, old clergymen – charming companions, but a lowering diet when prolonged.

Last year I went to Central Africa, but saw nothing. I flew there and back and spent a month in purely English circumstances cross-examining authorities on the book I was writing. Africa again without preoccupations with eyes reopened to the exotic. That's the ticket.

January 1959.   Ticket? Not altogether easy. This is the season when the ships are fullest. The wise man sails before Christmas. A visit to the Union Castle office in London. They are able to offer a cabin in *Rhodesia Castle* at the end of the month. She is a one-class ship sailing on the eastward route through the Suez Canal, stopping at several places I knew in other days and will gladly revisit, and reaching Dar-es-Salaam on 20th February. On 27th March their new flag-ship, *Pendennis Castle*, leaves Cape Town on her fast return voyage to England. That leaves me exactly five weeks in which to wander down by land.

I am told I shall need an inoculation against Yellow Fever and that under the new medical organization this cannot be given by one's own doctor. Instead one must visit a city. In London a nurse was giving, it seemed, some thirty shots an hour at a guinea a time. I purchased my certificate there. In the course of my journey I crossed many frontiers, but no government official ever asked to see it. The only person to show any concern for my health was the ticket clerk at a tiny airfield in Tanganyika. Medical authorities seem to have grown tamer lately. I remember great annoyance at the hands of the captain of a Belgian lake steamer crossing to the Congo in 1931; who sent me ashore under a blazing sun to find a doctor on a golf links who, as the hooter was sounding for departure, certified my immunity from a variety of contagious diseases. As for the nineteenth century, which is popularly supposed to have been so free, readers of Charles Waterton may remember that in 1841 he was shipwrecked on a voyage from Civita Vecchia to Leghorn and with his fellow-passengers obliged to transfer to the ship with which they had collided. When they reached Leghorn they were refused permission to land by the quarantine authorities on the grounds that their original bill of health had gone down with their ship. Only the impassioned intervention of Prince Charles Napoleon saved them from twenty days' incarceration. It is wrong to represent bureaucracy as an evil contrived solely by socialists. It is one of the evidences of original sin. The great alluring false promise of the socialists is that the State will wither away.

When I tell people of my movements, they say either: 'Not a very pleasant time to be going. Everything will be very disturbed after the Accra Conference', or 'A very interesting time to be going. Everything will be full of life after the Accra Conference'. No one, when one is going to Paris, warns one of the dangers from Algerian terrorists or envies one the excitements of UNESCO. As a defence I pretend to an interest in archaeology. 'I want to have a look at the Persian vestiges in the off-shore islands.' I like showy ruins and am moderately knowledgeable about European architecture, but I can't distinguish periods or races in Mohammedan building. I mean to go to some of these 'off-shore islands' (what is an in-shore island?) if I can. I am grateful to them for turning many conversations from the 'colour problem' and African nationalism.

January 27th. A friend in London gave a dinner-party to wish me a good journey and kindly assembled people she thought I should like to see. I was put in mind of Swift's observation: 'When we are old our friends find it difficult to please us, and are less concern'd whether we be pleas'd or no.'

An odious and graceless thought; a wintry thought; high time to be off.

January 28th. It is satisfactory to leave for the tropics in bitter, dingy weather. Sometimes I have left in sun and new snow and felt sorry to be off. I am taking the train to Genoa and boarding my ship there. At Dover no one looked at our luggage or passports, but we were none the less herded into the ritual procession round the customs shed. Why can't the train draw up alongside the ship as at Calais? There are lines laid to the quay. The great majority of the passengers carry their own bags and have a long, unnecessary march.

Ticket troubles at Calais. The train comprises miscellaneous sleeping-cars bound for various destinations; only one for Rome and that full. I have to travel in the Simplon-Orient which leaves Paris later than the Rome Express without a dining-car and shall have to change trains in the early morning at Milan. The conductor and guard assure me that they have information that all sleepers are engaged on the Rome Express.

Paris at the cocktail hour. How gaily I used to jump into a taxi and visit the bars while the train crawled round the *ceinture*. Nowadays, hard of hearing and stiff in the joints, I sit glumly in my compartment. At the Gare de Lyon there is an hour in which to try and change to the Rome Express. Clearly a case of 'où est le Cooks homme?'. The wagon-lit office is shut, but a Dickensian figure in the peaked cap of a travel agency lurks near it. He falls into a hoarse disquisition about a rebate I can get by avoiding Swiss territory, if I get the *chef de train* – 'chef de train mind – conducteur won't do –' to endorse my ticket and send it to the issuing agency. I persuade the Agent that this is not the primary problem. He pads along with me to the platforms. In the hazy evening the station is an ant heap of sleeping-cars scurrying in all directions. My car has disappeared with my luggage. We find an empty berth on the Rome Express, then that car too wanders abruptly away into the darkness while I am talking to the conductor. 'Oh, so you speak French, eh?' says the Agent resentfully as though I had been imposing on his good nature under false pretences. No porters in view – 'Ah porters, now, you don't see many of them these days.' The Agent, who seems as rheumatic as I, limps off to find one. I stay at the Rome Express platform, where my sleeping-car presently returns and is immediately overrun by Indians, men, women and children all beautifully dressed and talking volubly in English. They fill corridor, steps and platform. Five minutes to go and the Agent appears among them with a porter and my baggage. 'What I haven't got, that's your tickets. Conducteur wouldn't hand them over.' He indicates that our transactions are finished. His tip is bigger than he expected (or deserved) and he leaves me with a faint hint of geniality. Precisely at 8 the conductor from my first train comes swimming through the surge of Indians with my tickets. The train moves and suddenly all the Indians start tumbling out of it, leaving one dapper, waving sweetly-scented couple.

I wonder what Cooks-homme's history is. His French sounded very French to me; his English was the kind of cockney one seldom hears nowadays in London. Most of what I said struck him as densely obscure. An English soldier left over from the first World War perhaps, who had married a French girl and settled down with her? A Frenchman who had worked some years in a British colony and picked up the language of his mates? As happier men watch birds, I watch men. They are less attractive but more various.

Man-watching at dinner. The second service is pleasantly unfrequented. A striking figure sits opposite me, hirsute and swarthy; a Syrian revolutionary? an unfrocked Coptic clergyman? He addresses me in English. I take a shot and he admits to being a Sikh who cut his hair and shaved his beard in Detroit. He is now growing them again, but they will not yet have reached a suitable length when he meets his family. How will they take it? I mention the assembly of Indians at the station and surmise they were diplomats. There are no diplomats in Detroit, the Sikh says; everyone works hard there. Then he gives me a detailed account of his sufferings from the avarice of French taxi-drivers. I tell him he will find things worse in Naples, where he is going. He is stopping on the way at Rome. Is that a good place? He knows nothing whatever about it except that it is the capital of Italy. He has never heard of the Caesars, of the Popes, of Michelangelo or even of Mussolini. He is an engineer and, I suppose, about thirty years old and quite well off.

January 29th. Genoa shortly before 8. I have a friend whom I have more than once attempted to portray in fiction under the name of 'Mrs Stitch'. Mrs Stitch was wintering in Rome and I had told her I was coming to

Genoa on the remote chance that she might join me. The main reason for my anxiety to get into the Rome Express was that I should be at the hotel at the time I had told her. Just as I finished shaving after my bath she turned up with four hats, six changes of clothes and a list of complicated chores for her friends, for whom she habitually recovers lost property, books tickets and collects peculiar articles of commerce.

Her first business was at the railway station which, for a reason that was never clear to me, was harbouring a coat of unlovely squalor abandoned somewhere by one of her more irresponsible cronies. Without authority or means of identification Mrs Stitch cajoled a series of beaming officials and possessed herself of the sordid garment. 'How different from the French,' Mrs Stitch said, '*they* would never have let me have it.' I sometimes suspect that one of the reasons she gets on so badly with the French is that she speaks their language well. In Italy she has to rely purely on her looks and always gets her way without argument.

Breakfast in the station. The one perennial dissension between Mrs Stitch and me is that I like to eat in marble halls under lofty chandeliers while Mrs Stitch insists on candlelit garrets and cellars. She thinks my preference hopelessly middle-class and tells me I am like Arnold Bennett. Mrs Stitch's greatest difficulty in Italy is that there are singularly few quiet, murky restaurants; the smaller they are, the noisier and the more brilliantly lighted. The railway station at Genoa provided a happy compromise. For luncheon we found what Mrs Stitch wanted at Olivo's on the old quay. At dinner at Pichin in the new quarter the cooking was admirable but the light blinding. On the second day we drove out to a gay little beach restaurant at Nervi. I was never able to get her into the restaurant of our hotel and wistfully caught only an occasional glimpse of its sumptuous Victor-Emanuel trappings. The cooking of Genoa, like its architecture, is mild-flavoured and wholesome.

From this generalization I exclude the Campo Santo which for the amateur of cemeteries is one of the Wonders of the modern world. We went there at once and emerged after two hours dazed by its preposterous splendours. When the Genoese lost their independence, the energies that had once taken them on piratical hazards into unknown waters, and the remains of their accumulated wealth, were devoted to the private commemoration of their dead.

We are accustomed to the grandiose tombs of monarchs and national heroes. In Genoa for more than a hundred years professional and mercantile families competed in raising purely domestic temples. They stand round two great quadrangles and extend along the terraced hillside beginning with the strong echo of Canova and ending in a whisper of Mestrovic and Epstein. They are of marble and bronze, massively and intricately contrived. Draped and half-draped figures symbolic of mourning and hope stand in unembarrassed intimacy with portrait-sculptures of uncanny realism. There stand the dead in the changing fashions of a century, the men whiskered, frock-coated, bespectacled, the women in bustles and lace shawls and feathered bonnets, every button and bootlace precisely reproduced, and over all has drifted the fine grey dust of a neighbouring quarry. 'He's taken silk all right', said Mrs Stitch before a gowned barrister, and indeed that is precisely the effect of the dust that has settled in the hollows of the polished white marble. All appear to be lined, flesh and clothing alike, in grey shot-silk.

There are *tableaux* almost *vivants* in which marble angels of consolation emerge from bronze gates to whisper to the kneeling bereaved. In one group there is a double illusion; a marble mother lifts her child to kiss the marble bust of his father. In the 1880s the hand of *art nouveau* softens the sharp chiselling. There is nothing built after 1918 to interest the connoisseur. It is as a museum of mid-nineteenth-century bourgeois art in the full, true sense, that the Campo Santo of Genoa stands supreme. If Père la Chaise and the Albert Memorial were obliterated, the loss would be negligible as long as this great repository survives.

Fortunately it was untouched, or apparently so, in the bombardments of the second World War. It was reported in 1944 that the city was 'flat'. Some fine buildings were irreparably lost, but today, apart from an unexploded British naval shell that it gratefully exhibited in the Cathedral, there is little evidence of damage. I remember when Italy declared war on us in 1940, a politician exultantly proclaiming on the wireless that we should soon add notably to ruins for which that country was so justly famous. (It is worth recalling that before the surrender of Rome the English wished to destroy it and were prevented only by our American allies.) He did not take account of the Italian's genius for restoration. They do not, as do those in authority in England, regard the destruction of a good building as a welcome opportunity to erect something really ugly in its place. They set to work patiently exercising the arts of their ancestors. The palaces and churches of Genoa were, it seems, in ruins in 1945. Now walking the streets with Augustus Hare's guide book of 1875 Mrs Stitch and I could see almost all that he saw, as he saw it.

I did not know Genoa before the war. I went through by owl-light countless times, but the train runs underground and one gets no glimpse of the city's beauties. It is a place much neglected by English and American sight-seers who hurry through on their way to Rome and Florence and Venice. Genoa cannot be compared with these. It has no stupendous works of art and is haunted by few illustrious ghosts. It is stately and rather prosaic and passes almost unnoticed in the incomparable riches of Italy. In another country it would be the focus of aesthetic excitement.

All that is interesting, apart from the Campo Santa, lies in the little triangle between the two railway stations and the water-front. There one may see two streets of palaces and some thirty churches displaying every phase of architecture from early mediaeval to late rococo. The palaces are all, I think, in public hands or divided into offices and flats. The shipping agency, where I went to verify my sailing, is housed in a delicate eighteenth-century building whose gates lead into a *cortile* with beyond it, through the further arch a hanging garden rising into the sunlight on elaborately sculptured terraces. The two important streets, the Via Balbi and the Via Nuova, unpleasantly renamed Via Garibaldi, are narrow and deeply shaded except on the roofs and upper storeys, where at dawn and sunset the pediments and cornices reveal their strength. The doorways are immense and through them beyond the quadrangles and open stair-cases there is often a bright view, on one side of the sea, on the other of the mountains. Steep populous alleys lead down to the harbour, but they are clean and sweet. The people are as polite as Romans. There are no child-beggars, only the traditional, black robed, bead-telling old people on the steps of the churches. The Genoese of the old city go to bed early. After dinner one can prom-enade the empty streets finding at every corner a lamp-lit shrine and meeting few motor-cars.

The chief hotel stands near the railway station. Luggage is carried there through a tunnel under the traffic, which during the day is thick and fast. It is as good an hotel as I have found anywhere. As I have said, I was not allowed to try the cooking; everything I did try was first-class, in particular the two concierges. When one is travelling, one's comfort depends more on concierges than on cooks or managers or head waiters. These functionaries are getting rather rare in England and are quite unknown in America. Outside Europe they tend to be rascals. There is in England a Corps of Commissionaires, who have their own burial ground at Brookwood. They are fine figures, uniformed and bemedalled, who have cost me a lot of sixpences in my time. Concierges, on the other hand, have to be polyglot, omniscient, imperturbable as croupiers, patient as nuns, and endowed with memories as deep and accurate as librarians. Mrs Stitch has some of the requisite qualities, but not all. I should be the worst possible man for the job. The concierges of Genoa romantically assumed that my meeting with Mrs Stitch was clandestine and showed exquisite tact in defending our privacy and concealing our identities from an enquirer whom they took for a private detective. I should like to believe that there is an international corps of concierges, a Sovereign Order like the Knights of Malta, and a splendid cemetery where they can all lie together at the end, but I am told they never resort together and mostly retire quite young and rather rich and blandly fatten ducks in remote, soft valleys.

Mrs Stitch and I took our sight-seeing easy. One night in a wagon-lit did not work in me any miracle of rejuvenation. I was not yet good for more than two miles a day, nor could I eat more than a spoonful or two of the delicious confections of fish that were put before us. I was the same seedy old man who had groaned up to Paddington. But my eyes were opening. For months they had ceased to see; I had moved like a blind man through the lanes and hamlets of Somerset and the familiar little area of London that lies between the London Library and the Hyde Park Hotel. I needed a strong draught to quicken my faculty, and I found it in the Counter-Reformation extravagance of the Gesu. That picked me up and I was ready for the subtler beauties of the Cathedral.

My hope, not I trust wholly presumptuous, in publishing this diary is that the things which amused and interested me on my little tour may amuse and interest some others. I do not attempt to guide them by enumerating all the objects to be seen, nor even all I saw. E. V. Lucas's 'Wanderer' series of descriptions of famous towns, which give so beguiling an air of leisure, of the sensitive eye freely roaming, of mature meditation of unhurried feet pottering, of the mind richly stored with history and anecdote, were in fact, his daughter has revealed, the fruit of breakneck speed and frantic jottings of the kind most ridiculed in less adroit tourists. During these two days in Genoa I hobbled along beside Mrs Stitch, popped into places that looked interesting, sat down as often as possible and stared hard; and my vision cleared. I was not to see much of architectural beauty during my tour, but I brought to other spectacles eyes sharpened on the stones of Italy.

One little puzzle I met which has often exercised me since. For centuries the most illustrious relic in the very rich treasury of San Lorenzo (it claims also the ashes of St John the Baptist and has furnished them with superb vehicles for exposition and procession) was the Sacro Catino. It is a large dish of green glass, broken and put together with a small piece missing, and handsomely mounted. It is displayed in the treasury still, but the sacristan makes no claims to its authenticity. It has an old history. In 1101 Genoese and Pisan crusaders sacked Caesarea. The loot was enormous, but the Genoese happily surrendered all their share in exchange for this dish which local pundits assured them was used by Our Lord at the Last Supper for washing the apostles' feet. More than this it was cut from a single prodigious emerald which Solomon had given to the Queen of Sheba.

The Genoese bore it back in triumph, enshrined it and protected it as the greatest possession of the republic. Twelve knights were appointed to the high honour of holding the key of its casket for a month each, year after year. In 1476 a law was passed making it a capital offence to try alchemical experiments with it. So it was guarded and venerated until the Revolution. In 1809 French free-thinkers captured the city and bore the Sacro Catino off to Paris with other treasures. In 1815 it was restored, but on the road between Turin and Genoa someone dropped it and broke it and plainly revealed that it was made of glass. By an inexplicable process of the human reason the Genoese at once decided that it was totally spurious. If it was not the Queen of Sheba's emerald, it was not Our Lord's basin. No knights guard it now. It is displayed to profane eyes as an *objet de vertu* among the silver altar fronts and the Byzantine reliquaries, all beautifully arranged and lighted as though in the Victoria and Albert Museum.

After luncheon on the second day I covered my suit-cases with the gummy labels of the steamship line and lay down to read. After half an hour I was disturbed by a series of strange noises, cracklings and rustlings. Every one of the labels, whether attached to leather or canvas, was detaching itself and rolling up into a little cylinder. Rum.

Farewell, Mrs Stitch. She returned to Rome with the gruesome coat on her elegant arm.

2 · Voyage

Embarkation – Port Said – Aden – English at Sea –
Americans in Africa

January 31*st.* The *Rhodesia Castle* is a clean, seaworthy,
punctual ship with a swimming-pool, cinema-screen and
all modern amenities, but no pretensions to *grand luxe.*
The food was abundant and seductively named and
seemed to cause general satisfaction. I cannot say much
about it. I was treating this voyage as a cure. A ship is
one of the few places where one can play the ascetic
without causing annoyance to anyone else. Accordingly
I subsisted chiefly on fruit and cold ham. I never entered
the bar, where the jollier passengers forgathered, and
eventually landed in Africa lighter and very much more
agile than I had embarked.

The ship was quite full and I was lucky to get a cabin
with a bathroom. Not that I can find much use for a bath
at sea. A ship is as clean as a hospital; except after days
on shore, washing is a formality; for the first days of hot
weather the fresh-water shower is a pleasure; after that
the cold water runs hot and one breaks into sweat anew
as one tries to dry. But throughout the voyage I compared the privacy and spaciousness of this journey with
the squalor of my flight the year before.

At the time of writing (July 1959) there is a correspondence in *The Times* about the horrors of third-class air-travel. I had gone to Rhodesia first class. Perhaps we were objects of envy in our expensive quarters, but we had little compassion to spare for the second-class victims forward. We had our own bitter troubles. It was impossible to sleep and very difficult to get to the lavatory. After dark it was a strain to read by the little spot lights. All of us, rich and poor alike, were periodically turned out to wait for refuelling at airports which ingeniously contrived the utmost gloom with the utmost restlessness. There was nothing to do but drink. It took days to recover.

Looking round the miscellaneous shipping in Genoa harbour, I ponder another contrast. Here are vessels of all ages, many of them shabby and battered, all doing their work safely and surely; unlike aeroplanes which capriciously develop what the engineers prettily dub 'metal fatigue' and incinerate their occupants.

Sunday, February 1st. There are three priests on board, Dutch, Italian and Irish-American, on their way to different mission stations. Also two parties of nuns, Catholic and Anglican. The Anglicans are put out that they are denied Communion, but they hear Mass regularly. The Anglican nuns were unmistakably English spinsters. None of them had developed that round cheerful face whose expression varies from serenity to fatuity which one sees everywhere in Catholic convents. These

Anglican sisters are universally respected in Africa for their good works. They did not seem notably joyous. But who am I, of all people, to complain about that?

Most of the passengers came on board at London and have made up their bridge fours and dining tables and generally got acquainted, so that I am able to study them in solitude. I had expected a predominance of elderly people of the kind one finds on the banana boats in the West Indies, making the round trip for their rheumatism or bronchitis. There are some of these, but very few. The great majority are the young, returning to work; not adventurers seeking a fortune; not, at this late age of Africa, empire builders; but the employees of governments and big commercial firms taking up secure posts as clerks and schoolmasters and conservators of soil; sons of the Welfare State; well qualified, well behaved, enjoying an easy bonhomie with the stewards. Many have young wives, children and infants in arms.

A printed notice proclaims: 'The Captain and his officers will wear Blue Mess Kit White Mess Kit Blue Uniform White Uniform at dinner tonight' with the inapplicable words struck out, but few take advantage of this hint. Mine is one of a dozen dinner-jackets worn in the evening.

The library is reserved for adults. It is also free of wireless. Instead of a single, fatigable orchestra, most ships nowadays have loud-speakers everywhere and the succession of gramophone records is only interrupted by announcements – test match scores, geographical and meteorological information from the bridge, news of the ship's recreations. (One exhortation on this voyage was enjoyable: 'At 12.45 today a passenger was observed throwing a basket-chair overboard from the verandah. If this is an expression of dissatisfaction, the Captain would like the opportunity to put things right.') The library is a place of refuge. It is also well stocked with some thousand books of which I possess a dozen only and have read a further two dozen. The steward tells me that the Line employs a professional librarian who visits every ship at London and Southampton and distributes books. He must have a peculiarly difficult task, and he does it admirably. Every taste finds some satisfaction. For me a voyage is the time to read about the places for which I am bound and to study the best-sellers of the past year. I got through two books a day and never found myself without something readable.

February 3rd. The Mediterranean is cool and calm. Clocks go on an hour. Sir Harold Nicolson has said that he resents this shortening of his life. I find it exhilarating; the gift of a whole precious hour totally free of delinquency and boredom. Odd that traditionally the voyage west, where days and nights get longer and longer, should symbolize the expedition to the Fortunate Isles.

Found Maurice Baring's 'C' in the library which I have never read. It was written in the same room with Ronald Knox; he and Maurice typed together in the library at Beaufort; one so meticulous, the other so slap-dash. The discrepancies in 'C' are startling. Did he never re-read what he wrote? Are his devotees thrown into a trance by his gentle melancholy and rendered quite unobservant? The distance of a country house from Oxford varies from page to page between nine and six miles. Still odder one of the leading characters, Mrs Evelyn, appears first as an elderly widow, then as married and middle-aged, then as a siren, the mistress of Leila's husband and is in her final apotheosis 'the essence of London'. Maurice's delicious spontaneity, versatility and humility, that made him one of the most lovable of men, are not the attributes of an artist, who is more often crabbed and assiduous and touchy and jealous and generally unclubbable.

February 4th. Port Said at dawn. Over a hundred dauntless passengers left for the gruelling dash to the Sphinx and to Suez. I did not land. The officials who came on board wore khaki service dress and Brodrick caps. No tarboushes to be seen. The touts have discarded their white gowns for shoddy western suits, exemplifying the almost universal rule that 'Nationalists' obliterate national idiosyncrasies. Even the 'gully-gully' man wore trousers.

I have often wondered about the history of these performers, more comedians than conjurers, who, as far as I know, are peculiar to the Canal. Few tourists in these days go shopping in Port Said or sit in its cafés. (I remember the days when everyone going out, male and female, bought a topee at the quayside and those returning to Europe from the tropics threw them overboard in the basin to be scavenged by Arab boatmen.) So nowadays the 'gully-gully' men ply between Port Said and

Suez, boarding the ships and giving performances on deck at advertised times. I first saw them in February 1929 when perforce I spent some weeks in the port. Their repertoire is as immutable as the D'Oyley Carte's. The craft, I have been told, is hereditary. The man who squatted on the deck of the *Rhodesia Castle* must be the son of one of those whose attentions in 1929 became rather tedious after long repetition; or perhaps he was one of those tiny children whom I mentioned in a book called *Labels*. 'There was a little Arab girl,' I noted, 'who had taught herself to imitate them perfectly, only, with a rare instinct for the elimination of essentials, she used not to bother about the conjuring at all, but would scramble from table to table in the cafés, saying "Gully-Gully" and taking a chicken in and out of a little cloth bag. She was every bit as amusing as the grown-ups and made just as much money.'

There is a distinctly military tinge about the gully-gully ritual, which dates perhaps from 1915, much facetious saluting and the address: 'Oh, you, officer, sir,' when chickens are produced from waistcoat pockets. There is also the invocation of the name of Mrs Cornwallis-West derived from a remote and forgotten scandal. But who began the art, when? Most Oriental and African conjurers assume converse with the supernatural. No doubt Egyptian conjurers did a hundred years ago. Some unrecorded Charlie Chaplin or Grock of the water-front must at about the time of *Aida* have first hit on the idea of introducing farce; perhaps the literal progenitor of all gully-gully men. I wish I knew.

All day in the Canal drifting past the dullest landscape in the world, while the passengers hang fascinated on the taffrails and take spools of snapshots.

I remember once seeing a soldier of the French Foreign Legion desert, jump overboard just before luncheon, and stand rather stupidly in the sand watching the ship sail on without him. Once much later, during the last war, I remember a happy evening on the Canal dining with two sailors whose task was to employ numberless Arab bomb-watchers. When they reported an enemy areoplane and a splash, traffic was stopped until the missile was found. The clever Italians, I was told, dropped blocks of salt which dissolved, leaving no trace. Divers worked for days in vain searching for them and the Canal was blocked as effectively as by high explosive. But there was nothing of interest during this day's journey. All one could see was a line of behinds as the passengers gazed and photographed nothing.

The Captain tells me he finds the Canal the most interesting part of his voyage.

The weather grows pleasantly warm; not warm enough to justify the outbreak of shorts which both sexes, from now on, inelegantly assume.

February 6th. A cool, fresh breeze down the Red Sea. For an Englishman the English make ideal travelling companions. I have been accosted twice only; once by a woman who took me for my brother, Alec, and again by a man who mysteriously claimed to have been at Cambridge with Ronald Knox.

The constant music, I suppose, caused genuine pleasure to five per cent. of the passengers; pain to one per cent; a vague sense of well-being to fifty per cent.; the rest do not notice it.

February 8th.—Anchored off Steamer Point, Aden, after luncheon. The ship stays until midnight. A bazaar is set up on a raft below the gangway. Launches ply to and from the quay.

Since I was last here Aden has grown green; not very green, but there are distinct patches of foliage where there was only dust. We originally occupied Berbera, in Somaliland across the straits, in order to have somewhere to grow cabbages and fruit for the garrison of Aden. Water has at last been struck and piped. The continuous trains of shabby camels no longer pad along the road from Crater Town. There are taps and water-closets now in the settlement. I saw only one camel and that was a sleek riding animal from up country, sitting beside its master at an Arab café feeding on a hamper of green vegetables.

Most of the passengers drove off to see the water-tanks ascribed to King Solomon. In a thousand years' time, will Central African guides show tourists the mighty ruins of the Kariba dam as one of the works of Solomon? I wish I could think so.

I took a taxi to Crater Town and walked its narrow streets for an hour looking for remembered landmarks and finding none. Not that there has been much modernization, but things have disappeared. I could find no trace of the 'Padre Sahib's Bungalow' where I once spent a week. Nor of Mr Besse's emporium. I was Mr Besse's guest on several occasions in his rooms above his offices and warehouse. I also went with him on an appalling climb to the edge of the crater and across the burning volcanic debris to his shark-infested bathing-beach on the far side of the little peninsula. He was an enchanting man. I described him in a book called *Remote People* as 'Mr Leblanc', and was told later that he greatly relished the portrait. I wish he had shown his gratification by leaving me something. He was a rich man then. His great fortune came later and I was astounded ten years ago to read that he left £2,000,000 to Oxford University, an institution which can never have caused him a moment's pleasure. I do not know what he was by race or religion. They named the college he founded St Anthony's, but, when I enquired here, no one knew or had troubled to conjecture which of the twelve canonized Anthonies they were commemorating.

The smells of Crater Town are unchanged – spices, woodsmoke, coffee, incense, goats, delicious Arab and Indian kitchen smells, garlic and curry, sewage and hair oil. It is always a wonder to me that the English who cheerfully endure the reek of their own country – silage, spaniels, cabbages, diesel fumes, deodorizers, fish and chips, gaspers, ice cream – fight shy of 'native' streets.

Wireless rang out everywhere, I suppose from Cairo. There were portraits of Nasser in many of the Arab shops.

Back to Steamer Point. Here there has settled all the tourist trade which used to flourish in Port Said, but in a sadly standardized form. Simon Arzt's in the 1920s was richly cosmopolitan. You could find most of the luxuries of Europe there. At Aden the shops are all kept by Indians and each has an identical stock of Japanese counterfeits – 'American' fountain pens, 'Swiss' watches, 'French' scent, 'German' binoculars. I searched for cigars, but found none. There used to be two hotels at the extremes of the crescent. Their verandahs were haunted by touts and money-changers and shirt-tailors, and each possessed a 'mermaid' – a stuffed manatee, I think – which was kept in a chest and exhibited on payment. Now one of these hotels had gone and in its place has arisen a large, modern, air-conditioned building; no place for a mermaid. The other is its old shabby self.

I had a personal interest in the mermaids, because six years ago I suffered briefly from hallucinations in the course of which I imagined myself to be in communication with a girl in Aden. She complained of having nothing to do there. I went into some detail (which I omitted from the account I wrote of the experience) about the rather limited diversions of the settlement. Among them I mentioned the mermaid. 'It's gone, Evelyn, it's gone,' she said later, in tones of reproach as though I had maliciously sought to raise false hopes of pleasure, 'it isn't here any more.'

I was curious to discover whether in this particular as in all others my 'voices' had been deceiving me. But here she spoke the plain truth. The first servant I addressed at the hotel looked blank and shrugged, supposing I was demanding some exotic drink. But a much older man came forward. 'Mermaid finish,' he said.

'How?'

'One man came finish mermaid.'

'When?'

'Not so long.'

The curse of Babel frustrated further enquiries. I should have liked to know how the mermaid was finished – bought, stolen, destroyed by a drunk? – and particularly when it disappeared – before or after or even during my conversations with my forlorn confidante?

9th February. In the Gulf of Aden we lost the breeze which kept us cool in the Red Sea. Once round Cape Guardafui we are in the steam-bath of a New York heat-wave. It is more agreeable and, surely, healthier to come to the tropics gradually than to be deposited there suddenly by an aeroplane in the clothes one wore shivering a few hours before in London.

A great stripping of clothes among the passengers. Cortes marched from Vera Cruz in armour; Stanley crossed Africa in knickerbockers and a braided tunic; I in my humble way have suffered for decency. I have worn starched shirts at Christmas dinners in both Zanzibar and Georgetown, British Guiana; but these young people must be almost naked in order to lie in deck-chairs in the shade. The thighs of middle-aged women quiver horribly at the library-steward's table. How different the three Arabs we have taken on board at Aden, who are travelling to Zanzibar. They wear the light cotton robes of their people and always look cool and elegant and clean. They sit playing dominoes in the smoking-room and three times a day spread little mats on deck, take off their sandals and prostrate themselves in prayer.

I have found a diverting book named *Stars and Stripes in Africa; Being a History of American Achievements in Africa by Explorers, Missionaries, Pirates, Adventurers, Hunters, Miners, Merchants, Scientists, Soldiers, Showmen, Engineers and others with some account of Africans who have played a part in American affairs*, by Eric Rosenthal, 1938.

It begins rather surprisingly with Columbus, who once put into the Gold Coast. Some Americans believe he discovered the United States, but can many, I wonder, suppose he flew the Stars and Stripes? Mr Rosenthal was injudicious only in his choice of title; perhaps his publishers chose it for him; American publishers are more presumptuous than European in these ways; anyway, the sub-title fully explains his achievement. He rejoices to trace every connexion, however tenuous, between the two continents and has produced a fascinating collection of uncommon information. In fact, I think, the only time that the Stars and Stripes were taken into Africa was at the head of Stanley's expedition to Livingstone (who appears here among American worthies on the grounds that one of his sons died after the battle of Gettysburg; he had enlisted in the Federal army under an assumed name, was wounded and taken prisoner. It is not quite clear from Mr Rosenthal's account whether he fought in the battle.)

Americans have every excuse for claiming Stanley as a compatriot. He claimed it vehemently himself and was at one brief period a naturalized citizen. But he was born and died a Briton. He was the illegitimate son of Welsh parents, jumped his ship at New Orleans, enlisted in and deserted from both sides in the Civil War. When he became widely advertised and was invited to explain his origins, he hesitated between the embarrassments of admitting his illegitimate birth and his 'illegal entry'. He then formally abjured his country. When he became respectable, rich and married he re-naturalized himself British, sat in Parliament and was knighted.

It is interesting to learn from Mr Rosenthal of the enthusiasm of individual Americans for the establishment of the 'colonialism' in Africa which their grandchildren reprobate. At the time of the Boer War, he tells us – I was about to write in the manner of a book-review, 'he reminds us'; I had no idea of this or of most of the facts he adduces – Theodore Roosevelt wrote to Selous: 'the most melancholy element in the problem is what you bring out [in the *Spectator*] about Englishmen no longer colonizing in the way Boers do'.

In the invasion of Matabeleland in 1893 it was a young American trooper, Burnham, who hoisted the Union Jack over Lobengula's Kraal and three years afterwards his father, Frederick Burnham, later chief Boy Scout of the U.S.A., contributed to the pacification of the area and won loud applause by bringing in the head of what he described as 'the M'Limo'. It was a large claim. The M'Limo is an ancient African deity worshipped and consulted in the Matopo Hills long before the coming of the Matabele and still revered as far south as Bechuanaland; his priests are drawn from the Kalanga tribe; they make rain and pronounce oracles. Burnham, 'at stupendous risk', as Mr Rosenthal remarks, had bagged one of these.

There were eight American members of the Reform Committee in Johannesburg who first invited and then repudiated the Jameson Raid. One of them, Hammond, was condemned to death but later with his fellows was bought off for £25,000 a head.

A Philadelphian built the first synogogue in Rhodesia.

These and many other facts I have learned from Mr Rosenthal. The most moving narration is of the efforts made in 1900 to solve the problem of the Boers by wholesale evacuation. The Governor of Arkansas offered 5,000,000 acres of his State as a free gift. Colorado followed suit. In Wyoming 300,000 acres were actually irrigated and planted for the Boer immigrants. If these farsighted and generous policies had been realized, much annoyance would have been spared Her Majesty's loyal subjects.

February 10*th*.   A fancy-dress ball. The general aim is to be comic rather than seductive. Some jokes are purely verbal – a dress sewn with used matches patiently collected from the ship's ash-trays and labelled: 'No more Strikes'. Many beefy young men assume female clothes with balloon breasts. One of them wears nothing but a towel fastened like a baby's napkin and is pushed round the dance floor by another dressed as a nurse. He carries a large feeding-bottle and the inscription: 'Beer builds bonnie babies'. An elderly woman with whitened face parades in a sheet festooned with empty gin and whisky bottles. She represents 'Departed Spirits'.

For a great many passengers this party celebrates the end of the voyage and the end of leave. We are due at Mombasa on 13th, where they disembark and go to work in Kenya and Uganda.

3 · Voyage Continued

Mombasa – Kenyan hospitality – Officials and settlers –
Fort Jesus – Gedi – Kibo – Tanga – Zanzibar

February 13*th.*   The *Rhodesia Castle* spends five days in
Mombasa. Few passengers stay on board during this hot
season. I had made no plans and knew nobody in the
colony. Nearly all my old Kenya friends have died, some
by suicide, or returned to their homelands. (The generous,
genial, unconventional population of the highlands was
by no means exclusively British. There were Americans,
Danes, Swedes, French, many of whom used their Kenya
estates as holiday resorts.) Nairobi, I was told, is now
unfriendly, huge and infested by thieves; the care-free life
of the Muthaiga Club is a memory; rather a scandalous
one. A second generation of farmers has grown up with
their own social habits, provincial in experience and
opinions, more industrious than their predecessors in the
Happy Valley, but not such good company. This is the
opinion I was given on the *Rhodesia Castle*. It sounds
plausible enough. There was nothing in the Kenya I knew
to suggest that it enjoyed any immunity to change. Why
should not this equatorial Arcadia, so lately and lightly
colonized, go the way of Europe? I did not seek to verify

it. I could not hope to see much in five days. Besides, the Queen Mother was in progress up country and I surmised that casual trippers might not be particularly welcome at that time. But in Mombasa, at any rate, I found that the old tradition of open hospitality flourished as it used to up country.

A former neighbour of mine in Gloucestershire had served in the Sappers with a friend now settled in Tanganyika. He wrote to report my imminent arrival. This second sapper not only, as will appear, made himself my host and companion in Tanganyika, he wrote to a third sapper, a highly placed official in Mombasa who came on board the *Rhodesia Castle* with the passport officers, introduced himself and took charge of me with a bounty which is often called 'oriental' but in my experience is particularly African. I was the friend of a friend of a friend and I didn't know anyone in Mombasa, so that was enough for him to lend me his car and his driver, take me to a tailor and to a watchmaker, ask me to luncheon at his home, put me up for his club, advise me about anti-malarial specifics, introduce me to the Provincial Commissioner and the Director of Antiquities and perform all the other kindnesses that I shall shortly record.

In my last visit to Kenya I met few officials. There was a rigid apartheid between them and the settlers, who looked on them almost as enemy agents. Those were the days of the Hartington declaration of policy; that where the interests of the immigrant and native races conflicted, the interests of the natives were 'paramount'. If this had been said by a Socialist Colonial Secretary, it would have passed unnoticed; coming from a Tory (and a future duke), it made the settlers for the first time 'politically-conscious'. They saw the Colonial Office as their declared enemy who sought to rob them of the lands they had cleared and ploughed and watered. The officials, they said, had no stake on the country; they were in transit, thinking only of promotion and pension; they would retire to die in Europe. The settlers were transforming a wilderness where they intended to found families. (Come to think of it, I never heard much hostile criticism of the rich cosmopolitans on these grounds.) There was a popular story at the time of a district officer who seduced a farmer's child and begot twins. He honourably offered marriage. The farmer said: 'I would sooner have two bastards in my family than one official.' I daresay it is a very old story that has been told of Montagus and Capulets, Campbells and Macdonalds for generations. But I first heard it of Kenya during the 'paramountcy' agitation.

All that bitterness seems now to have subsided. There was then a simple division between two groups of Englishmen, one trying to run the country as a Montessori School, the other as a league of feudal estates, each sincerely believing that it understood better the natives, and knew what was best for them. There was then a single, troublesome, alien element comprised of Indians. No one talked of African 'Nationalism'. Now officials, settlers and Indians have a common uncertainty of their future, and since the Mau-Mau 'emergency' no one pretends to understand the natives. (The suppression of that movement, I was assured by an officer closely concerned with it, was achieved by loyal or mercenary Kikuyus more than by regular forces.)

The city of Mombasa has grown enormously since I last saw it and now covers the whole island. There is a large brand-new 'interracial' hotel. 'Interracial' in practice means mainly Indian, for few Africans can afford it and the Europeans forgather in their houses or at the Club. There is an impressive Muslim Institute, erected by the late Aga Khan and the Sultan of Zanzibar and other pious benefactors for the technical education of East African Mohammedans. (The Government of Kenya provide the staff and the running expenses.) They were unusually fortunate in their architect, Captain G. N. Beaumont, an engineer amateur of Mohammedan art who is splendidly uncorrupted by the influence of Corbusier which pervades the modern east. Dome, minaret, arcade, fretted and crenellated parapets, carved doors, tiled walls and pools stand happily disposed in acres of garden, whispering hints of the Alhambra, of Mena House, of the Anglican Cathedral at Gibraltar, of Brighton, but never the harsh tones of UNO.

These two buildings are the chief architectural additions to the city. There is evidence of what seems to be the universal process of offices becoming larger and private houses smaller. For the first time in Africa I heard complaints of the scarcity and expense of domestic servants. The population of the island is more than ever heterogeneous. There are now poor whites in quite formidable numbers – a thing unknown 30 years ago. There is also in the main street a notorious dancing-bar, part brothel, part thieves' kitchen; everyone spoke of it with awe. When at length after many invitations I found a companion to go there, I found it the genuine thing; not at all the tourists' apache café, but something which awoke nostalgic memories of the Vieux Port of Marseilles. All races and all vices were catered for. I have never been in a tougher or more lively joint anywhere. Gentle readers should keep clear.

Kilindini docks are now enormous and efficient. Everywhere there was every sign of prosperity (I suppose complaints about domestic servants are one of these signs) and of political tranquillity.

I have here run away from my diary and given the impressions of several days. On the day I am ostensibly chronicling I spent a restful afternoon on the club verandah with the intention of reading the news I had missed since leaving England. The club is unchanged since I was last here, a spacious, old-fashioned building designed to catch every breath of air. The monsoon was blowing. It was deliciously cool, but it is not easy to read *The Times* India paper edition in deep shade and a brisk wind. Have the editors, I wonder, considered what a high proportion of their copies are perused under fans?

Opposite the club stands one of the most notable buildings in East Africa, Fort Jesus, built by the Portuguese at the end of the sixteenth century and still bearing the royal escutcheon on its walls. Its base is cut from the rock; its upper stories are faced with hard, coral stucco which changes colour as the sun moves over it, mottled, sometimes dun, sometimes rose-red. It is a massive little castle sited for defence on all fronts, battlemented, pierced by slits, approached by a single narrow flight of steep enfiladed steps. Until lately it was used as a prison and all the visitor could see of it were its noble elevations. He could smell it, when the wind was in the wrong quarter from the club verandah. Now, by means of a grant from the Gulbenkian Foundation, it is being cleaned and restored. By the time that these words appear it will be open to view, furnished with a collection of local antiquities and, more important, inhabited by Mr Kirkman, the official archaeologist, who has been in charge of the operation.

At 5 o'clock that evening the fort was at its rosiest under the full blaze of the westering sun when, through the kindness of my new sapper friend, I had an appointment with Mr Kirkman. Few people in Mombasa had had the chance to see the work in progress, and a privileged party of six or seven assembled at the gate and were led up to the ramparts. There is nothing of the dry and solemn official scholar in Mr. Kirkman. He is an exuberant enthusiast for the comic as well as for the scientific aspects of his work.

The Public Works Department had built over the old structure a shoddy conglomeration of guard-rooms, cells, latrines, barrack-rooms, wash-houses and exercise yards. All these were being demolished and the original levels were being restored. The Arabs had left a few finely carved inscriptions, but what emerges from the excavation is essentially a Portuguese Government House of the seventeenth century. Mr Kirkman gleefully recounted the history of the settlement which is in microcosm the history of the East African coast from Cape Guardafui to Sofala.

Few of the leading figures led enviable lives. The Arabs were the first comers to the island. In the sixteenth century the Portuguese set up a small trading station under the protection of the Sultan of Mombasa but relying for its defence primarily on an alliance with the Sultan of Malindi. In 1588 a Turkish pirate raided and sacked the coast. The Sultan of Mombasa appealed to Constantinople, the Sultan of Malindi to Goa. The Sultan of Mombasa then decamped. Later the Turk reappeared and occupied the island as a base for attacking Malindi. A fleet was sent against him from Goa. Meanwhile, for several years a ferocious cannibal tribe from south of the Zambesi, called the Zimba, had been making a leisurely progress up the coast, eating their way through the inhabitants. They appeared on the mainland just as the Portuguese fleet anchored off the island. The Turks invited the Zimba to cross over and help against the Portuguese. The Zimba came, ate the Turks and, gorged, shambled away to the north, leaving Mombasa to the Portuguese. They were repulsed at Malindi and disappeared from history.

In 1591 the Portuguese began work on Fort Jesus. It was so attractive that their old ally of Malindi invited himself to stay. His hosts unkindly turned him out and bought his head from the mainland villagers with whom he took refuge. When this deed was reported in Lisbon and Goa, the royal authorities were shocked. It was decided that in reparation the Sultan's son Yussuf, then seven years old, should be educated and Christianized. In 1630 he turned up again at Mombasa in European clothes with a white wife under the name of Don Jeronimo. His reception was not as cordial as he had hoped and he began to regret the simplicities of the faith of his fathers, so at a party given in Fort Jesus he arranged a successful massacre of all Christians. It was his last success. He wandered away first to the Yemen, then to Madagascar and was finally murdered by pirates in the Red Sea. The Portuguese reoccupied Fort Jesus until it fell to the Arabs of Oman. The siege from 1696 to 1698 is one of the memorable feats of human endurance; at the end the garrison was reduced to eleven men and two women. The Governor was so tortured by skin disease that he chose to attack the enemy sword in hand. The relief fleet arrived a day late.

In the next century the Portuguese re-took the Fort and held it for a year. It fell to the Muscat Arabs whose representative, the Sultan of Zanzibar, is still the titular ruler. Visitors who see a red flag flying there need not fear un-American activities. It is the Sultan's own standard. The British Protectorate was established after being anticipated by a droll episode in 1824 when a captain of the Royal Navy intervened, at the Sultan of Zanzibar's request, to put down a rising of his subjects on the coast. At that time, while the main body was employed on the mainland, Fort Jesus was commanded by a midshipman. A small civil war broke out under the walls of the fort. The boy sent a stern warning to both sides that unless they desisted, the combatants would be punished 'with all the forces at his command'. They desisted. The forces available at Fort Jesus at the time were five Royal Marines, two of whom were down with fever. The protectorate so light-heartedly proclaimed was repudiated by the home government. General Gordon entertained the whimsical notion of annexing Mombasa to Egypt. It was not until 1887 that British administration was established. There is no record of any African having ever ruled there.

This vivid little history was conveyed to us as we stood on the battlements with infectious but inimitable zest by the Director of Antiquities.

That evening I dined with the Provincial Commissioner. Like everyone I met in Mombasa that day and later he was in a daze of gratification at the Queen Mother's visit. On every occasion she had done more than was asked of her. Unflagging in the steam-heat, she had completely defeated the boycott the politicians had tried to impose. In particular, she had made a conquest of the Arab sailors whose dhows fill the old port at this season. Nasser's wireless had been denouncing her as the symbol of Western imperialism. Dhows came sailing in from Zanzibar and all the little ports of the coast. The Queen Mother went to the water-front and paid them a long, happy call which will be talked of for years in the Hadramaut and in the Persian Gulf.

Politics do not seem to be a major concern in Mombasa. Much of our conversation that evening was about the prospects of developing the Kenya coast as a holiday resort. There are sands, surf, coral reefs, deep-sea fishing for marlin, tunny and shark, an almost unexplored sea-bed for goggle divers, everything in fact that draws tourists to the West Indies. At present Mombasa is used mainly as a port and rail-head; rich sportsmen go straight to Nairobi and set out on safari from there into the game reserves. The Commissioner hopes to see his province become a pleasure coast, not only for visitors from Europe and America but for families from the highlands of Kenya and Rhodesia. Rhodesians at present tend to take their holidays at sea-level which doctors recommend, at Durban, a salubrious but unromantic and expensive city. In the cool months Kenya has far greater natural attractions.

February 14th. Today I was able to see something of these attractions. But first I had to make arrangements to sleep out. Nights in the ship tied up alongside the quay at this season are barely supportable for their heat and the noise of stevedores. But deliverance came in the form of a Frenchwoman of incongruous elegance; she · came aboard the moment we docked, dressed in a uniform of her own designing, the representative of her husband's travel agency, the very antithesis of the Agent at the Gare de Lyon. All yesterday she had been despatching parties of animal-watchers into the interior. She was on duty again this morning, spruce and cool. To her sympathetic ear I disclosed my insomnious problems and she at once, for rather a lot of money, arranged for me to sleep the next two nights at a place named Kibo on the slopes of Kilimanjaro.

But first a jaunt up the coast; at 10 o'clock my sapper friend and his wife called for me at the docks. We picked up Mrs Kirkman at her hotel and drove north over the ferry to the mainland. We crossed with a handful of girls from a neighbouring tribe whose name sounded like Gujama. Amid the slatternly European fashions of Mombasa these pagans still preserve their African grace, bare to the waist, prettily tattooed and decorated with wire and beads. The road north runs through alternations of bush and village plantations of coconut and corn. A few independently minded Europeans live in small-holdings cleared from the bush near the ferry. In one of these Mr Kirkman was staying. He joined our party and we drove past Freetown, a settlement of slaves freed in the last century, to the ruined city of Gedi.

Current guide-books still speak of this as overgrown and shunned by the natives for fear of the ghosts who abound there. This was true ten years ago, but today much of it has been cleared and some of it excavated. It was Mr Kirkman's first task in Africa. For those who lack the archaeologist's constructive imagination and are not easily moved by the contemplation of stratified debris, Gedi is second only to Zimbabwe in charm and mystery. It was abandoned, not destroyed; its dilapidation has been from natural causes, storm and invading vegetation during the centuries in which superstition protected it from men.

It was a large, double-walled Arab city, probably founded in the twelfth century. No one, not even Mr Kirkman, knows why it was built here, so far from the sea. Arab geographers refer to the 'iron mines of Melinde' (Malandi). It may have had some connexion with this industry. It is conceivable that the river Sabaki may once have run to the sea below its walls and that it was a depot for trade with the interior. No one knows why it was suddenly deserted in mid-sixteenth century. Perhaps the Zimba paused and sustained themselves there in the course of their gluttonous migration. Anyway, there is plenty to interest the sight-seer who is not a specialist, arches, streets, six mosques, a palace, three pillar tombs, six mansions complete with bathrooms and privies, water supplies, drainage, store-rooms and courts, all of the fifteenth century, when it seems to have been completely rebuilt. There is a market and coffee-shop. Porcelain and stone-ware from China, glass-ware and beads from Persia have been unearthed. There is still much to be found, but it is easy enough already to picture the populous, prosperous and pious community which flourished there in its period of greatness. The natives now show no reluctance to take part in the work of exhumation.

Two Swahili families are permanently quartered there as custodians. The women were preparing a meal, a horrible mess of mealies. There has been no improvement in the basic East African diet in the last twenty years. As we are constantly reminded, most Africans are always underfed. Poverty, of course, is the true origin but not always the immediate cause of their wretched food. Most of them, I am told, when they are in funds – on returning, for example, from spells of work in the mines – prefer to spend on showy clothes or strong drink. They enjoy an occasional glut of meat when an animal has been killed, but they have no taste for the balanced and varied diet which the health officers would like to inculcate.

There is no recognizable trace now of the once powerful Sultanate of Malindi, where we drove for luncheon. There is instead a pretty little seaside resort with an excellent beach hotel decorated in the style derived from Rex Whistler.

That evening I went with the captain of the *Rhodesia Castle* to dine with the Union Castle agent. The party was mainly of Mombasa businessmen and their wives. It was clear that the enthusiasm aroused by the Queen Mother's visit was not confined to officials. All spoke of the notorious Star Bar, but none had been there and I could prevail on none to go with me.

February 15th. Set off early on the road to Kibo. A party from the *Rhodesia Castle* were away before me, packed tight in the cars, under the guidance of the English husband of the elegant French travel agent. I self-indulgently had a big car on my own with a driver from the Chagga tribe who live round Kilimanjaro. As will appear later, the Chagga are a remarkable people, very much more civilized than their neighbours.

The road follows the line of the railway, which is itself

the old caravan route to the lakes. Wherever you find old mango trees in East Africa, you are on the Arab slave-tracks. It is a hot, dull road and I was glad to be alone. At noon we came to Voi – the entrance to the game reserve which had attracted my fellow-passengers. Mid-day is no time for animal watching. At dawn and dusk the bush comes to life. We drove slowly round one of the many routes. Under the glare of the sun the area seemed empty and dead; high, dry, dun grass; low, colourless scrub; here and there small trees uprooted by elephants, ash-white as though struck by lightning. Every few minutes we stopped and my driver dramatically pointed to a colourless swift-moving object in the middle distance – a buck or impala or dik-dik. He had sharp, practised eyes and his regular run was to this Park to show wild life to tourists. I am both ignorant and blasé about tropical fauna. At one time or another I have been at close quarters with most sorts of big game. Baboons seem to me far less interesting than, say, the Gujama women on the ferry yesterday. I disappointed my driver by my languid attention and my insistence on getting to the hotel before the larger and keener party, whom we passed gazing intently at some giraffes. They were spending the night at Voi in order to see the elephants come out to drink at sun-down.

They arrived at the hotel as I was finishing luncheon and went up to their rooms to sleep; I drove on to Kibo.

A breathless, hot road crossing and recrossing the branch railway line. Nothing of interest on either side. Somewhere on the way we crossed the frontier from

Kenya into Tanganyika. There was no police post. No one asked whether I had lately been vaccinated. A few Indian shops round a railway station; then we turned off to the right and began to climb. Within a mile we had reached a different country. The summit of Kilimanjaro was hidden in cloud. All we saw was the green slope of gardens merging into forest. On either side of the lane grew coffee and bananas behind flowering hedges. Sweat dried and the air became cool and thin. At the end of our journey was a small, solid, old-fashioned German hotel, with balconies, a terrace, a lawn, flower garden and a cage of monkeys. The inhabitants of the hotel were youngish European couples, some with children, some it seemed on their honeymoons, but in the evening the terrace became more cosmopolitan. Indians are not allowed to settle in this area, but a motor-party came from Moshi and drank fruit juice. Three parties of local Chagga very well dressed and well behaved came to drink beer.

I slept under a blanket and woke in the exhilaration of the mountain dawn.

February 16*th*. Kilimanjaro was visible in the morning, a snowy camel's hump. Explorers of the last century wrote lyrically of this huge, odd, dead volcano that rises out of the plain. It looks less than its height, perhaps because of the high level of vegetation. From the hotel at Kibo parties set out from time to time to climb it. There are rest-huts for the nights and the tramp is made in three days. Ropes and axes are not needed. It is a heavy walk, not a feat of mountaineering, but many strong men fail in the last lap, overcome by mountain sickness. The successive belts of vegetation are a joy to the botanist.

I spent the day with my driver, who was happy to be at home and proud to act as guide. At every turn we met friends and relations of his. I shall have more to say of the Chagga later, the most prosperous and intelligent of the native peoples of East Africa. The Germans gave them security against their war-like neighbours, Catholic and Lutheran missionaries and a revered commissioner named Charles Douglas taught them the arts of peace, but before the white man appeared they had shown themselves an ingenious people, excavating deep caves for refuge from slave-traders and building a stone-walled canal which follows a valley contour and irrigates a village ten miles distant. Many streams from the snow-line fall in green fringed cascades to be lost in the torrid plain below. It is a scene of theatrical charm. Save for its sturdy black inhabitants it might be in Polynesia. Then into this arcadia there came strolling two elegant, arrogant old men, each dressed in a single cotton length, very tall, upright and slender. 'Masai', said my driver in the voice he had used to point out the game in the reserve, but with an unmistakable note of fear in it, as though he were warning me of something more dangerous than beautiful, for it is not fifty years since the Masai used to raid here and drive the Chagga literally underground, and the memory survives. These two men had come in from their lands beyond the mountain on a peaceful errand, carrying long wands instead of spears, to visit a doctor; but their shadows cast a brief gloom as they passed.

At lunch-time the other tourists from the *Rhodesia Castle* arrived at Kibo. They had been out at the watering-places in the reserve at dusk and dawn, had seen many animals and taken many photographs, and were well content with their experie1ces.

February 17*th.* Back to Mombasa. That night I found a jolly, bearded doctor who was willing to go with me to the Star Bar. It was his first visit and it was he who decided after a very few minutes that it was no place for us, after a girl from Zanzibar who, he diagnosed, was intoxicated with hashish, had taken an unreasonable and demonstrative dislike to his benign appearance. I must admit I was enjoying it awfully.

February 18*th.* Sailed at dawn and put in at Tanga for the day. I remained on board as I intended to go there later from Dar-es-Salaam, but I may here give advice to those who find themselves, as we did, with a day to spend in this busy provincial capital.

Don't let them take you on a sisal estate unless you have some peculiar interest in this vegetable, which was clearly intended by nature to be a picturesque weed; planted in regular lines of seemingly limitless extent it is deeply depressing.

Don't let them take you to a sulphurous cave they are proud of.

The place to visit from Tanga is Pangani, an Arab town some thirty miles down the coast. There is a good road to it (after Pangani it ceases to be passable at most seasons) and two places of interest on the way, a ruined mosque at Tongoli, rather like all other ruined mosques to the untrained eye, and a Swiss-owned sisal estate quite unlike any other, in that a Swahili workman showed a taste for mural decoration and his employers have kept him, as it were, as their official artist. The village consists of identical rectangular white-washed, concrete habitations, arranged in lines, as practical and as drab as the rows of sisal that surround them. These walls are now almost totally covered with vivid, naïve life-sized scenes of local life – dancers, animals, white men, Indians, natives of various tribes, askaris, police, convicts. They are not painted to survive the centuries, but for the time being they provide a lively spectacle.

The village was full of loungers, many rather drunk, for a good workman can cut his stint of sisal in four hours and if he wishes stop work at ten in the morning, having earned all he needs for the day. If he does a second stint, he can afford great quantities of liquor.

Pangani stands at the mouth of the river of that name which rises on the southern slopes of Kilimanjaro. Opposite it, across a ferry where the road leads uncertainly to Dar-es-Salaam, there is bright green hill and an old mosque. On the Tanga side there is a fine waterfront and promenade, a grand Arab fort, now the District Commissioner's house and office and some tall, impenetrable Arab mansions where the descendants of the slave-traders and dhow-builders live their decadent lives. It is said that a mild form of domestic slavery still survives behind their blind white walls. A small hospital and prison, German built of local materials in the local manner, have a deceptive and agreeable air of antiquity. British occupation is commemorated by a tablet marking the place of a landing during the first World War and by two nasty little buildings erected by the Public Works Department. No European lives there except the Commissioner, and few Indians. There is a 'Lucky Bar' where the younger and more decadent Arabs openly defy the precept of the Prophet. They are said to be weak in intellect and deplorable in morals.

That is all there is to see at Pangani, but it is well worth a visit. Perhaps it will not survive long. It has no function in modern Africa. Should I scruple to disturb its gentle decay by recommending it to tourists? I don't think so. There are no gracious dreams in its present tranquillity. In its heyday the place was cruel and grasping and philistine. There is only physical beauty here and that of a low order – the picturesque. Let it be a target for cameras.

February 19*th.* There has been a change in the character of the passengers. The missionaries and officials and many of the young men going to work got off at Mombasa and were replaced by holiday-makers, many of them from remote Kenyan farms who come down for a few days cruise to enjoy a change of diet and of company.

We anchored off Zanzibar at dawn. A day of fierce heat. The island is said to enjoy a cool season. I have never struck it. An hour's stroll ashore sufficed to revive old memories; then I retired to the ship for a cold bath and an afternoon under the electric fans.

To elderly Englishmen Zanzibar is most famous for the great Bloomsbury rag, when Virginia Woolf and her friends inspected an English man-of-war at Portsmouth in the guise of the Sultan and his entourage, and for Bishop Weston's occupation of the Anglican see. Weston was the hero of many sermons in Lancing chapel and his cathedral, built on the site of the old slave-market, the symbol of British beneficence in East Africa. Weston it was who, just before the first World War, threatened a schism in the Church of England by delating his neighbouring bishops for collaboration with nonconformists. Readers of Ronald Knox's *A Spiritual Aeneid* will remember the intense excitement of his coterie about the incident which, he said, the Lambeth committee found 'eminently pleasing to God and on no account to be repeated'. The Cathedral has a rather forlorn appearance today. One clergyman presides where there was a 'mess' of six. The main activities of the mission are now on the mainland and the historic little edifice has, with its brass plates commemorating British officials, the air of a Riviera chaplaincy. No church has made much progress in this last of the Arab sultanates. Eighty years ago it was hoped that a province was being added to Christendom. British rule has merely created an Indian settlement.

It was ironic, too, to find notices in the ship and on the quay requesting European ladies to respect local susceptibilities by dressing modestly. Shades of Mrs Jellaby and of all the sewing parties who used to make 'Mother-

Hubbard' gowns to clothe the naked heathen! The French are said to be the most shameless tourists. Unless turned back by the police they parade the bazaar in 'Bikini' bathing dresses.

There are no beggars or touts in Zanzibar. The narrow lanes are clean and fragrant and shaded. I saw no changes except that the fort has been tidied and made public. It is a pretty town. Few buildings are more than 150 years old, but all are built in the traditional fashion of plastered rubble, painted and repainted, with here and there delicate blue washes relieving the mottled white, with carved doors and hidden gardens, and the streets wander along the paths first traced by pack animals. Besides the usual trash for tourists there are genuine Arab and African antiquities to be found in the shops. The money changers have vanished, who used to produce from their leather bags gold pieces struck all over the world and still current, priced by weight, whenever the Arab dhows put in port. A few trousered figures flick wads of escudos under the noses of passengers bound for Mozambique, where venerable, turbaned obesities once squatted by their scales. There is still no tourists' hotel. Magicians still frequent the north island of Pemba, coming from as far as the lakes for their final schools in the black art. The reigning Sultan succeeded in 1911 and has been on his throne longer than any living ruler. His subjects have no nationality, part Arab, part Indian, part Swahili; British administration is pure, effective and benevolent. No doubt we shall soon read in the papers about 'Zanzibar Nationalism' and colonial tyranny.

What I read in the papers now, at the moment of writing is this:

'One of Zanzibar's tourist attractions – the old stone town with its narrow streets and houses with intricately-carved Arab doors — is to be cleared partially to provide improved living conditions. The inhabitants will be moved to new areas where proper amenities can be provided.

'Part of the cleared area will be used for the development of warehouse space in the port area to encourage the establishment of new industries essential to the island's economy.

'The estimated cost of the scheme, which ensures the balanced progress of housing, communications, commerce, industry, education and all community services is £258,000, but only £58,000 can be allocated because of the lack of funds.'

The last sentence is comforting.

4 · Tanganyika

Dar-es-Salaam – Bagamoyo – an historic fiasco – Kilwa – the coronation of Bishop Homer A. Tomlinson

February 20th.   Dar-es-Salaam at dawn.

I made a grateful leave-taking with the *Rhodesia Castle*, where I had recovered from all the malaises of the English winter and landed in extreme heat in Tanganyika. Dar-es-Salaam, too, has its cool season during the English summer. Its most loyal citizen could not claim that the climate in February is pleasant. Nor that the city has much to divert the sight-seer; less than Mombasa, which it somewhat resembles; no Fort Jesus, no Star Bar. It is a port, a rail-head and the seat of government – unlike Mombasa it is the capital city, a distinction which means more every year as political institutions multiply. Its suburbs extend along pleasant beaches. There is sailing and fishing and a hospitable British society.

Tanganyika is a pure bureaucracy, the number of officials has doubled since 1945; they attempt to run a Welfare State on an exiguous budget. They regard themselves as temporary caretakers who will quite soon hand over their responsibilities to natives. The head of the 'Nationalist' movement, Mr Nyerere, is universally well spoken of (though 'nationality' in a people as hetero-geneous as those arbitrarily assigned to the territory has less meaning there than almost anywhere in the world). There are very few white settlers of the sort that abound in Kenya and Southern Rhodesia, a few farmers, mostly industrious Boers, round Arusha, a few reputedly eccentric English of the old 'Happy Valley' kind in the Southern Highlands. There are a few sisal estates owned by Greeks and Swiss. Over great areas the tsetse fly keeps man away. The great European settlement was made by the Germans at the turn of the century. They were evicted in the first World War. In the 1930s the Germans began to return. They were very uppish, openly making lists of chiefs they would hang when Hitler recovered the land for them. (It was never properly part of the British Empire but a territory held under mandate of the League of Nations.) In 1937 it seemed quite probable he would succeed. The history of Africa and perhaps of Europe would have been very different had he done so. In September 1939 the British authorities neatly arrested the lot, taking them quite by surprise, and interned them for the duration of the war. There are very few of them in the territory now. Whenever one finds a building of any attraction, it usually turns out to be German.

One of these was the Club, where I was kindly lodged. It stands on the sea-front behind a broad terrace. In the time of the German occupation it had a beer-hall, skittle-alley and an adjoining brothel. Now there is instead an excellent library. There are a very few air-conditioned offices in Dar-es-Salaam. The older buildings are designed to catch the breeze. The Dar-es-Salaam Club is solidly built with much fine joinery in dark African timber and heavy brass fittings on doors and windows. In the days I spent there I sat for many hours sitting under the fans, sipping lime-juice (curiously enough limes are almost unprocurable in Tanganyika outside the capital. The hotel managers say, as they do in England, that there is 'no demand' for them) and reading the best-sellers of the last decade. It was very much like being on board ship. At sun-down the Club came to life. Tables were set out on the terrace. Women appeared. Sometimes a band played. Shorts gave place to suits.

During the day the officials, who are the main white population, wear white shorts and open shirts, looking like grotesquely overgrown little boys who have not yet qualified for the first eleven at their private schools. Those who wish to add a touch of dandyism to this unimposing uniform sport monocles. I wonder how much the loss of European prestige in hot countries is connected with the craven preference for comfort over dignity.

At Dar-es-Salaam I met the ex-sapper to whom I had originally carried an introduction, and who at 400 miles' range had befriended me in Mombasa. He received me with urbane warmth. I will call him R. To him and to Mr Thompson, the agent of the Union Castle Line, were due almost all the pleasure and interest of my weeks in the territory.

Saturday, February 21st. A policeman has been murdered in the suburbs because his neighbours thought a witch was enjoying police protection. That, at least, is the current story. I saw a great customs shed full of elephant tusks and rhinoceros horns, all for export to India. In order to discourage poaching, which nonetheless is prevalent, it is forbidden to work ivory in Tanganyika. The elephant tusks fetch 18s. a pound, the rhino horns 60s. Most of the latter are eventually sent to inflame the passions of the Chinese.

February 22nd. Mass at the Cathedral (another German building), very full, mostly of brilliantly endimanchés Goans, hardly a white face to be seen.

R. drove me out to Bagamoyo, forty-five miles up the coast, to lunch with the government archaeologist, a young man not so effervescently happy as his confrère at Mombasa. In R.'s Mercedes-Benz we covered the very bad road in an hour and a half. Word had gone before me of my zest for ruined mosques. There are two – one mediaeval, the other of the eighteenth-century – some little distance from the present town, which is an agreeable decrepit nineteenth-century place, part German colonial, part Arab-slaver, with the spurious air of greater antiquity typical of the coast. The archaeologist has a charming house built in the traditional materials – a sharp contrast to a row of mean concrete villas lately erected for official occupation by the Public Works Department.

Bagamoyo was the starting-point of most of the missionaries and explorers of the last century. The Germans made it their headquarters before they developed Dar-es-Salaam. It will be remembered in history as the scene of a disastrous dinner-party given on 4th December 1859 to welcome the return of Stanley and Emin Pasha.

Every feature of Stanley's last expedition was tragic and villainous, tempered only by farce. Stanley himself in *In Darkest Africa* suggests diabolic interference.

Emin, it will be remembered, was a protégé of General Gordon's, who sent him to govern, in the name of the Khedive of Egypt, the equatorial province (to which Egypt had no claim) south of the Sudan. When Gordon fell, Emin remained beleaguered but for a time unmolested. Gordon had picked him up locally and little was known of him in Europe. He was a most likeable man, generous, gentle, deeply versed in natural history, a doting father to his half-caste daughter, but not quite the paladin which the English newspapers made of him. Born a German Jew, he worshipped indifferently in synagogue, church and mosque. He represented himself at times as a Turkish subject, at times as an Egyptian; he seems to have considered becoming both British and Belgian. He had a Turkish wife (deserted in Prussia) and an Abyssinian mistress. Emin was a name he adopted in preference to his patronymic, Schnitzer.

When he found himself cut off, he contrived to send appeals for help addressed to the Egyptian, British and German governments. Private enterprise responded. In 1886 a Relief Fund was opened and generously supported from a medley of motives, humane, patriotic and commercial. The betrayal of Gordon at Khartoum must not be repeated. Gordon's last lieutenant was represented as gallantly holding out against the hordes of the Mahdi with a handful of devoted troops. They must either be brought to safety or reinforced and rearmed to continue their defence. Also, there were a number of North Country business-men who were curious about the resources of central Africa, who thought the King of the Belgians had been sharp in snapping up the Congo and were eager to emulate him. An expedition through unexplored country meant a series of treaties and concessions from local potentates that could be turned to profit. Stanley had done it before. He must do it again. He accepted the leadership of the expedition.

As is made clearer in other reports than in Stanley's own, his appearance on the shore of Lake Albert precipitated a mutiny in Emin's army, which was largely commanded by officers who had been sent south to expiate crimes. So far from waging a gallant rearguard action they were very comfortably settled with harems and slaves and grown fat on the spoils of the surrounding countryside. Those who maintained a semblance of loyalty to Emin did so because there were rumours of a relief force. Emin and his staff, smartly dressed, came down the lake in their steamship and found Stanley ragged and starving at the head of a small advanced party who under any other leadership would have been a rabble. He had to return to pick up what was left of his wrecked forces. The Egyptians promptly mutinied and arrested Emin. But the mutiny, in its turn, and the rumours of Stanley's failure provoked the first serious attack from the Sudanese. Suddenly the mutineers decided they would follow Emin anywhere out of range of the fuzzy-wuzzies. The enchanting story should be read at length (I have done so). It is amply documented and has been attractively summarized by Mr Byron Farwell in *The Man who Presumed*. I have given this little sketch in order to point the disaster of the Bagamoyo dinner-party.

Stanley arrived at the coast on 4th December 1889. Of the force of 708 who had started to relieve Emin 196 returned. No one seems to have troubled to count the Egyptians he had rescued. They set out in great numbers with their women and children and household furniture and they melted away on the road. Not all died. Some found villages to harbour them. Some 260 eventually reached Cairo. Controversy about Stanley's treatment of his white officers was long and bitter. But anyway Emin was safe. There had been sharp quarrels between them and much matter for mutual recrimination, but they were ostensibly friends and colleagues. Stanley had reason to hope that the Pasha would show his gratitude by entering either the British or the Belgium service.

The Germans in command at Bagamoyo gave them a great reception. Thirty-four Europeans sat down to dinner. It must, I think, have been in the present Boma, the government office, but it was not possible to identify it confidently from the wood-cut in *In Darkest Africa*. It was certainly in a large building of two stories with a balcony. Nowhere else in Bagamoyo seems a plausible alternative.

A superb scene for the cinematographer; a great German spread; fresh meat and fresh fish; lashings of champagne; the multitude of insects, all dear to Emin, expiring round the lamps; a naval band below; in the streets the surviving Zanzibari porters celebrating their return with an orgy; speeches, songs; congratulations in various tongues made a lingua franca by common conviviality. Emin moves beaming from place to place with a courteous word for everyone; sailors, soldiers, consuls, missionaries and the guests of honour; crimson Teutonic faces and thick necks predominate; a huge contrast to the yellow-bellies on the shores of Lake Albert, now littering the trail inland.

Presently the Pasha is absent. Other men have withdrawn from time to time. The party goes on. Then under the uproar word goes round. The Pasha has taken a header off the balcony. The Zanzibari dancers are stamping round his bloody corpse. It is not quite as bad as that, but it is odder in its sequel. He *has* taken a header and has been picked up for dead, blood oozing from his ears. He is unconscious. The medical men leave the table, but the party goes on.

The Governor of Equatoria is not dead. Perhaps it would suit the cinematographer better if he were. He lies in a coma for many days, and when he comes to his senses it is not Emin, it is not Schnitzer. It is something quite new in his history; he is a junker. He who has acknowledged the ancient thrones of Constantine and Suleiman, of David, of Pharaoh and Cleopatra even, indirectly, of Alfred and Victoria recognizes only the brand-new, upstart empire of the Hohenzollerns. A telegram from the Kaiser has done the trick. He renounces all previous loyalties and in due time sets off up country on the quest of treaties on which these transient powers are based. But he was not long happy in his new allegiance. 'Would I had died after my fall on the stones of Bagamoyo,' he wrote in October 1891. His eyesight began to fail. Next year his expedition was as wasted by disease as had been Stanley's. Sitting at his table in camp near the Lilu River, some day's march from Stanley Falls, peering blindly at his specimens of plants and birds, the Arab slavers of the district (who had been chiefly responsible for the collapse of Stanley's rear column) came in and unceremoniously cut his throat.

On the road back we passed a village dance. They would keep it up far into the night, drinking and drumming; a jolly, social party not like the ngomas I used to see, which always had a hint of magic and, it seemed, of menace.

February 23rd.   I do not regret my insincere expression of interest in mediaeval Arab ruins. It has taken me to some delightful places and introduced me to delightful people. Today I booked to fly to Kilwa. My resolution to eschew aeroplanes – like Belloc's to eschew trains on the *Path to Rome* – has had to be broken. The road is impassable at this season; a steamship plies from Mombasa but to take that would have extended the expedition by some three weeks and inflicted a visit of unbearable length on my kind hosts – for there is no hotel. Visitors must either bivouac or impose themselves as guests on the District Commissioner. So prejudice, now and later, had to be put aside and at noon I stepped into the suffocating little machine (which of course was late) bearing, what I was told would be acceptable, a leg of mutton frozen, when I put it in the rack, to the consistency of granite but soft as putty when I presented it to my hostess.

My destination is some 200 miles down the coast from Dar. There are three Kilwas – the island of Kilwa Kisiwani, all ruins now and a few huts; the sleepy little nineteenth-century town of Kilwa Kivinje, Arab and German built, eighteen miles to the north on the mainland; and Kilwa Masoko, the new boma, or administrative station, to which I was bound. The aeroplane stopped at Mafia Island, a flat grove of coconut and mangrove which attracts deep-sea fishermen. We passed the Rufigi delta where the wreck of a German warship has lain visible for forty years. The Kilwa airstrip is near the boma. Here I was met by the District Commissioner and his wife and carried off to their house. His isolated position gives him a larger measure of freedom from bureaucratic interference than is enjoyed by any of his colleagues in Tanganyika. With the help of two young district officers he governs 3,000 square miles of territory. Inland it is said, there are more elephants than tax-payers; the few villages are visited on foot in the old colonial style. There are three European bungalows at Kilwa Masoko, an office, a school, two Indian shops and a pier. It is to this pier that the boma owes its existence, for in the heady days of the 'Groundnuts Scheme' it was designed to be the rail-head for the produce of the still virgin bush. The D.C. himself is one of the few benefits of that scheme; the 'groundnutters' have a low reputation, largely I gather deserved, but there was among them an appreciable number of zealous and efficient officers from the army who came out full of the faith that they would be doing something to help feed the victims of the war. These were the first to realize that the scheme was fatuous; some returned to England, others, of whom my host was one, remained in Tanganyika to do valuable work in other services. His wife and he are an exhilarating couple, both devoted to their large, lonely territory, without any regrets for the social amenities of the towns.

February 24th. A narrow channel separates the boma from the island of Kilwa Kisiwani. We crossed early in the morning by motor-launch, embarking at the pier and wading ashore up the sandy beach. Once the Sultan of Kilwa ruled from Mafia in the north to Sofala (near the modern Beira) 900 miles to the south. It was by far the greatest of the East African sultanates. Now, with its neighbouring islands of Songo Mnara and Sanji ya Kati, it is inhabited by a few families of fishermen. The Persians probably came here first and set up a dynasty in the tenth century. It was under the Arabs of Oman that the place became great. The Portuguese came there at the beginning of the sixteenth century. In 1589 the Zimba ate all the inhabitants and left a waste that was irregularly re-occupied. Once, in the eighteenth century, it recovered some prosperity, again under the Oman Arabs. It then declined steadily until the last sultan was deported by the Sultan of Zanzibar in the middle of the last century.

Archaeologists, notably Sir Mortimer Wheeler and Fr. Gervase Matthew, have lately paid professional attention to the district. There is plenty to delight the mere sight-seer.

A very faint, inexpungible tinge of luxury lingers in this desolate island. The goats and the few tiny cows which pasture there have made glades and open spaces of park land between the trees whose flowers scent the steamy air as though in a Rothschild's greenhouse; gaudy little birds flash and call as they used to in the aviary at Hackwood. Phrases from Tennyson's Alcaics come uncertainly and not entirely aptly to mind. 'Me, rather, all that bowery loveliness'; there are no 'brooks of Eden mazily murmuring' on Kilwa, nor 'cedar arches'; but 'rich ambrosial ocean isle' and 'the stately palm woods whisper in odorous heights of even' are exact and might have been written here.

The buildings lie along the north shore opposite Kilwa Masoko. The most prominent is the most modern, an eighteenth-century Arab fort standing on Portuguese foundations, probably on the site of an earlier fort, for it is the obvious place for the defence of the harbour. A seemingly ancient carved wooden doorway is, in fact, dated 1807. Once there was a long wall along the seafront, but this has been washed away; the walls to landward survive in various stages of dilapidation with towers at intervals; in the centre the Sultan's palace, consisting of the long narrow rooms whose dimensions were determined by the available timber beams. There are traces of red paint and ornamental plaster. Outside the walls stand a small, domed mosque, and a much larger one called the 'Friday Mosque'. Domed mediaeval buildings are very rare in East Africa. Blue-glazed bowls have been set into the cupolas and the minarets. Beyond these mosques lie a cemetery, another mosque, more fortifications, a huge water-cistern and traces of many unidentified buildings. The only mosque in use is a humble shed which serves the present population of a few fishermen.

The only man of importance is a nonogenarian Dervish, on whom I was taken to call by the D.C. He looked like a black Father Christmas. His chief possession is a large, carved bed which is coveted by the museum at Dar. He was not using it that morning, but was recumbent in a low chair, unable to rise to greet us, but attended by a pretty girl who carried a baby he assured us proudly was his own. I once supposed that Dervishes employed themselves either in spinning like tops or in breaking British squares, but I have since looked them up in the encyclopaedia and learned that the term is so wide as to be almost meaningless; they can be orthodox, pantheistic, mystical, political, ascetic, orgiastic, magical, ecstatic; they can live as members of strict communities or as hermits or nomads, mendicants, scholars, revivalists – almost anything it seems.

While the D.C. was exchanging politenesses in Kiswahili I noticed over our host's head a framed picture of King George VI with an inscription signed by a former Governor in the name of His Majesty 'as a record of the valuable services rendered by him to his own Country and People and to the British Government in advancing the Moslem religion'. It seemed an odd tribute from the Defender of the Faith.

On saying good-bye, the genial old man produced from his bosom a hen's egg and presented it to me. That afternoon the D.C.'s wife had a sewing class on her verandah for the few native girls of the station.

February 25th. Drove to Kilwa Kivinje—well laid out, well planted, picturesque, decaying. There are no European inhabitants. An Englishman sometimes visits an office where he transacts business in mangrove bark. He was in fact my fellow-passenger from Dar and returned there with me on the next flight. An aged Swahili magistrate sat in the old German court-house. In the ramshackle little German hospital Indian doctors rather ironically displayed their meagre equipment. A few youths squatted on their door-steps playing the endless and unintelligible gambling game of dropping nuts very swiftly and earnestly on a board hollowed out for them as for marbles in solitaire. No crafts survive in the town except, among the women, very simple grass matting; the ancient woodcarvers are represented by a single clumsy joiner. There are a few Indian grocers and a pleasant little market of fish and vegetables. Meat is almost unprocurable; hence my offering of frozen mutton. It was a regrettable and much regretted decision to move the boma to Masoko. Anyone having business at headquarters has a walk of nearly forty miles. There is, I think, no unofficial wheeled

vehicle in the district. The D.C. and his wife knew everyone in the place and were plainly welcome at every door.
He had lately on his own initiative repaired the sea
wall, thus preserving a promenade dear to Arab social
tradition.

February 26th.   The aeroplane came in the morning to
take me back to Dar. There was in it a copy of that day's
East African Standard containing this paragraph: 'Bishop
Homer A. Tomlinson of New York, self-styled "King of
the World", flew into Dar-es-Salaam last night from
Salisbury. He is to crown himself King of Tanganyika
today. He intends to leave the New Africa Hotel at 10
a.m. and walk around the town for two hours crowning
himself on a suitable site at noon.'

This seemed a happy confirmation of the theme of
Eric Rosenthal's *Stars and Stripes in Africa* which had
beguiled my voyage out.

We landed at 11 o'clock. Mr Thompson met me at the
aerodrome. He had not heard of Bishop Homer A.
Tomlinson's assumption of sovereignty. We drove up
and down the main streets of the city looking for him and
making enquiries. His progress, if it had occurred, had
been unobserved. At noon we came to the New Africa
Hotel. This, the leading hotel, is near the Club, separated
from the water-front by a little public garden and a war
memorial. In the tropic noon the place was quite empty
except for half a dozen policemen and two journalists.
They were waiting for the Bishop, and we joined them
in the scanty shade.

I expected a flamboyant figure from Harlem. Instead there presently emerged from the hotel an elderly white man dressed in a blue kimono. He was unattended and somewhat encumbered by paraphernalia. He gave no indication of expecting any kind of ovation. As purposeful and recollected as a priest going to his altar to say Mass, the Bishop shuffled across under the blazing sun, opened a folding chair and sat down in the garden. The police, the two journalists, Mr Thompson and I collected round him. A representative of the local broadcasting organization appeared with a tape-recorder. The Bishop ignored him and like a priest or rather, perhaps, like a conjuror, began arranging his properties. He had a bible, a crown which seemed to be light and inexpensive, a flag, not – shade of Rosenthal! – the Stars and Stripes but something simple but unidentifiable of his own design of blue and white stars, and a bladder. The stuff of his little chair was slightly regal, a pattern of red and gold with ornamental tassels. He dropped the flag over his head as though preparing for a nap. Then he blew noisily into the bladder which proved to be an inflatable, plastic terrestrial globe. He blew hard and strong, but there was a puncture somewhere. It took the form of a wizened apple but not of a full sphere. After a few more puffs he despaired and laid it on the ground at his feet. Then he removed the flag from his head and began to address us in calm nasal tones.

He was, he said, the acknowledged leader of the largest religious body in the world about 100,000,000 strong to date. In 1923 he had received the call to be a bishop; in

1953 to be a king. He was the sovereign of fifty-two realms and proposed to complete his vocation by crowning himself in every state in the world, including Russia. Under his simple autarchy peace would be assured to all his subjects. He then prayed for the prosperity of Tanganyika, placed the crown on his head, collected his impedimenta and retired to the New Africa Hotel.

The temperature that day was 90°, humidity 100.

From time to time in the next few weeks I had news of him. The Sultan of Zanzibar did not welcome a rival in his dominions. He was forbidden to crown himself there. He got to Nairobi by air, but the immigration authorities of Kenya suspected him of subversive activities and would not let him leave the aerodrome. They would not even let him crown himself in the waiting-room.

5 · Tanganyika Continued

Safari – Morogoro – Groundnut Scheme – Dodoma –
Kondoa – Arusha – a visit to the Masai – Moshi – the
King of the Chagga – Soni – Tanga – the last of the
junkers – the Emergency – Iringa

Saturday, February 28th. R. has arranged his business so that I can accompany him on a long 'safari' – a term now used to designate a luxurious motor tour. He has been a racing driver in his time and his affection for his car is tender to the point of infatuation. It is a worthy object of devotion, a large, new, fast and extremely comfortable Mercedes-Benz.

R. has a fixed smile of fascination and an air of self-confidence rarely found in civil servants. He is a large, handsome euphoric man in early middle age, as near a dandy as local custom allows; a late comer to the colonial service. He has – or rather had for he has just been promoted – an office requiring great tact, patience and discretion. He is in charge of 'personnel'; that is to say of all postings in the government service; most dissensions, discontents and scandals come to him for treatment and part of his task is to make periodic tours of the 'bomas' and see that everyone is reasonably happy and sane. With us, engaged on some rather similar errand whose precise nature I never learned, is a retired brigadier; a regular soldier of imperturbable geniality. I don't know if they enjoyed my company. I certainly enjoyed theirs.

We set out in the early morning. If brigadiers have an occupational weakness, it is neurotic solicitude about their baggage. Not so our brigadier who was blithe and carefree. Indeed, as will appear later, he was deprived of a portfolio of highly confidential documents during our tour and accepted the loss with admirable equanimity.

We drove due west up the old slave-route, which is now the path of road and railway. A road heavy with wicked association. No one, I suppose except a zealot of some recondite natural science, can find much pleasure in the coastal plain of East Africa. We sped where, not very long ago, we should have met the caravans of yoked and ivory-laden captives. Plantation soon gave place to bush. It was pleasant to be out of Dar and it was quite joyfully that we reached Morogoro before noon. Here we lunched with the District Commissioner. The conversation was of witchcraft, political agitation, tax-evasion, big game and secret societies – the staple, engrossing topics that greet one anywhere up country in Africa. There is little at Morogoro except the boma, the railway station and a few Indian shops. Yes, I know, I ought to write 'Asian'; Pakistanis don't like to be called 'Indian' nowadays, but I grew up with a simple vocabulary in which 'Asian' did not exist and 'Asiatic' usually meant a sinister Chinaman. I hope this little book will not be banned (like the Oxford Dictionary) in Karachi as the result of my antiquated habits of speech. No offence is intended.

There were no problems at Morogoro for R. or the brigadier. We drove on refreshed, and late in the afternoon came to a huge clearing in the bush, 90,000 acres of grassland. This is all that remains of the Kongwa groundnuts plantation which twelve years ago was a topic of furious debate in London and of bitter recrimination in Africa. The Overseas Food Corporation ceased to exist in March 1955. The Tanganyika Agricultural Corporation is now engaged in saving what it can from the wreck. Some 9,000 head of cattle, in herds of 300, have been put in the care of Gogo families. These tribesmen have reverted to their former scanty dress and rebuilt their houses on the ancestral model, very low rectangles of mud, with flat roofs of turf. Three veterinary and administrative officials are the only white population. The cattle are healthy and may multiply. But the Sodom apple threatens to overrun the pasture if not constantly resisted. If the experts go, the grass will go with them.

At my request R. diverged from the main road to visit the once populous site. It was not easy to find. The roads of Kongwa are breaking up, the railway lines have been removed, the airstrip is overgrown. Few buildings remain, and those are up for sale. As we drove to the only inhabited bungalow, an Englishman came out to ask if we had come to buy the school hall, for the final failure on this disastrous scene has been that of a secondary boarding school, the only one in Tanganyika, which that month was reopening in the Southern Highlands after some scandalous goings-on at Kongwa.

On a slight rise stand the empty bungalows which were once called 'Millionaires' Row' and 'Easy Street', where the high officials lived in the intervals of flying to Dar and London; sad sheds with the weed growing high in their gardens. We made our way through the growth and peered through the windows at the empty little rooms. It was hard to conceive that they had ever been the object of derisive envy.

There are two excellent documents, *The Groundnut Affair* by the late Alan Wood, written in 1950, and a brief retrospective paper by Mr A. T. P. Seabrook, the Chief Administrative Officer of the Tanganyika Agricultural Corporation, written in 1957. Wood was a loyal socialist and Public Relations Officer in the early stages of the scheme. When he wrote there still seemed a chance of growing some nuts. When Mr Seabrook wrote, he counted the secondary school, which was now being dismantled under our eyes, as one of the positive gains to the territory.

There was no injustice in treating the fiasco as a matter of party politics. The scheme was conceived in an ideological haze, prematurely advertised as a specifically socialist achievement and unscrupulously defended in London when everyone in Africa knew it was indefensible. No one at the top made a penny out of it. The officials were underpaid and had in some cases given up better jobs to come. I well remember the indignation, some twenty years ago, of a foreign art expert who recounted to me in great detail the transaction by which the National Gallery had acquired a painting of doubtful authenticity. 'And all of them,' he concluded in disgust, 'the Director and his committee are gentlemen of private fortune. Not one of them received even a commission. It could not have happened in any other country.'

Africa has seen many great financial swindles. This was not one of them. The aim was benevolent; the provision of margarine for the undernourished people of Great Britain. The fault was pride; the hubris which leads elected persons to believe that a majority at the polls endues them with inordinate abilities.

Mr Strachey's plan was to clear 5,210,000 acres of virgin bush in 1947 which in 1950 would produce 600,000 tons of groundnuts. The total expenditure, spread over six years, was to be £24,000,000. The estimated profit was £10,000,000 a year. It does not require acute hindsight to discern something improbable in this calculation. In September 1948 the administrative heads of departments in Kongwa submitted a report expressing dismay at the progress of the venture. This was ignored. At the end of that year £18,000,000 had been spent and current expenses were £1,000,000 a month. No considerable quantity of groundnuts was ever produced; nor was there a need for them – they were piling up in mountains in West Africa needing only transport to make them available. Altogether, I believe, some £40,000,000 were squandered by the Overseas Food Corporation. Rival politicians had every reason to make a row about it.

But the imagination is moved by the human elements

of the story. The Labour Government conceived it as their duty as trustees of the native races to institute Trades Unions and sent salaried officials to teach them how to strike for higher pay. In the first year their efforts were rewarded. The Europeans working at Kongwa had to be enrolled as special constables and organized in armed patrols for the protection of themselves and their servants. Bands of African spearmen blocked the roads. The railway stopped running. The tractors lay idle. Police had to be brought in from Dodoma. The Union leaders were taken to prison and the strikers' demands remained unsatisfied.

Frantic supply officials saw enormous quantities of derelict army stores accumulate at Dar from the Philippine Islands, brought in unlisted lots, the useful and the useless inextricably confused.

The site at Kongwa had been selected for its emptiness. It was empty because it was waterless.

The encampment at Kongwa housed some 2,000 men and women from Great Britain and some 30,000 natives. Their presence among the simple Wagogo came near to dissolving tribal loyalties. Their high wages put up the price of food so that natives not employed by the scheme went hungry. Many of the natives who were attracted by the high wages left their own smallholdings uncultivated, so that less food was grown in the Territory than ever before. Large quantities were imported to feed those who were supposed to be exporters. It was even proposed to import bees into an area where bees were the principal natural terror, in order to pollinate the sunflowers (which died of drought anyway). A half of all the liquor imported into Tanganyika was consumed at Kongwa. It was a new experience for most natives to see Englishmen demonstratively drunk. It was new, also, to see them convicted of theft. Villages of prostitutes, who charged stupendous fees of five shillings or more, sprang up round the encampment. The hospital orderlies did an illicit trade in injections which they pretended cured syphilis. Thieves infested the stores and workshops. A firm official promise that first priority would be given to the erection of 1,000 African married quarters, resulted by the end of 1948 in 200, and those inferior to what were provided by the Greek sisal planters; respectable Africans refused to move their families into them on the grounds that Kongwa was a bad address. The equalitarian ideas of the home government found no sympathy in Africa. The infinitely graded social distinctions among the workers (there are seven recognized classes of Mauritians alone) came as a surprise to the English socialists. By the end of 1948 there was a turnover in the labour force of twenty per cent. per month.

The pity of it is that many of the original 'ground-nutters', like my host at Kilwa, had come out to Africa with high, altruistic motives. These mostly left Kongwa in the first two years. It is ironical now to read what Alan Wood (who himself resigned in protest at the obliquity of public utterances in London) wrote in 1950: 'I believe that in Africa, as in Europe, the only real reply to Communism will be Socialism. The best answer to the Africans who dream of Soviet Russia is to boast that the ground-

nut scheme can be as remarkable an experiment as anything done under the Five-Year Plans; that it is based on
some of the same principles, something new in Colonial
development, a huge co-operative venture not run for
private profit, which will eventually be run by the people
who are working for it; but which represents an advance
on anything in Russia, in that large-scale economic
planning is combined with political freedom.'

We turned back to the main road past traditional
villages of the Wagogo. The inhabitants waved cheerfully at us. The immigrants have all departed, leaving
them much as they were when Livingstone passed
through, but the richer for some fine cattle.

That night we slept at Dodoma at the railway hotel. It
is a railway town, scattered, unlovely, noisy.

Sunday, March 1st. R. goes out before breakfast to
visit his motor-car and brood over it fondly. I passed him
on my way to Mass at the shabby crowded little church.
When I returned he had breakfasted and was giving the
windscreen a final caress with chamois leather as atten-
tively as a character from Erle Stanley Gardner wiping
finger-prints from a telephone.

From Dodoma we drove north, blank bush on our
right, hills on our left, a seedy track, part of what was
once hopefully spoken of as the all-British route from the
Cape to Cairo. A hundred miles brought us to Kondoa,
a pretty oasis with an unfathomable spring, a German
fort and granary, Arab houses still largely inhabited by
Arabs, and a vertiginous suspension foot-bridge over

which daring District Officers have been known to drive their motor-bicycles. The Public Works Department is engaged on replacing the spacious and cool houses which the Germans built for their officials with the cramped, concrete structures which are mysteriously preferred by the authorities in Dar. The District Officer, a young man of an earlier and happier type than his contemporaries, still occupied one of the old houses, but his superior, the District Commissioner, had been moved to an ignoble little villa.

At Kondoa we saw the last of Arab influence until we returned to the coast. From there we had 150 miles to go to Arusha, the road climbing all the way through the Masai steppe, empty, open country; the only incidents on the road were occasional hutted camps of the P.W.D. and at Babati a bar frequented by Field Officers and plump, unbecomingly dressed women from the Seychelles.

Arusha is the provincial capital, a considerable town with two hotels, one of which seeks to attract by the claim to be exactly midway between Cape Town and Cairo. There is a small pocket of white farmers in the district, some of them immigrants from the Union of South Africa. Perhaps because it was Sunday evening they gave an air of festivity to the bar and lounge. The rather large European managerial staff mingled affably with them. I did not see any African or Indian customers. Dogs howled and scuffled under the windows at night. Can I say anything pleasant about this hotel? Yes, it stands in a cool place in a well-kept garden and it stocks some potable South African wines in good condition.

R. and the brigadier have a full day's official business before them. They introduce me to the Acting Provincial Commissioner, who very kindly offers to lend me one of his officers for an excursion among the Masai. It is my rare good fortune, he explains, to arrive at the time when there is a great assembly of this nation for the ceremonial initiation of elders.

The Masai are, I suppose, the most easily recognizable people in Africa. Their physical beauty and the extreme trouble they take to adorn it have popularized their photographs in geographical magazines and tourist advertisements all over the world. Every writer on East Africa has paid his tribute to their pride and courage. A generation back they still carried the long spear, hunted lion with it and defended their grazing rights over a huge region much of which is now the 'white highlands' of Kenya. They gleefully pointed out at the time of the Mau Mau rising that it was the English who introduced the supposedly docile Kikuyu into those lands and they enjoyed their small part in the pacification. For a generation they had been punished for raiding the Kikuyu; now they were paid to do so. The story is told that a patrol was sent out with orders to bring in any Kikuyu 'arms' they could find; next morning the commanding officer's tent was surrounded with a heap of severed limbs. Fighting, hunting and herding cattle, sheep and goats – but primarily cattle – are the only occupations suitable for a man. The Matabele, an equally brave people, when conquered, immediately became the servants of their conquerors. No one has ever made a servant of a Masai; nor were they ever conquered; they have been cheated a little, but they have always negotiated with the white man as equals. They employ a servile tribe as blacksmiths and themselves practise no crafts except those of the beauty parlour. Four Holy Ghost Fathers work among them, but by far the greater part remain pagan and polygamous. Nor have they been influenced by the Mohammedan missionaries who are making more converts than the Christians in some areas round the Lakes. At the time of writing, it is announced that they have elected a Catholic paramount chief. There was no paramount chief before; authority resided in an intricate system of local chiefs and elders; the new office is, I think, that of an ambassador rather than of a ruler. They have found it convenient to appoint an educated spokesman to deal for them, not so much with the British Commissioners who understand them, as with the educated Africans of other tribes who will shortly be assuming power; who would like to despise them because they do not wear shorts but have inherited an ineradicable awe. The Masai are not primitive in the way that pygmies and bushmen are. They are an intelligent people who have deliberately chosen to retain their own way of life. Tobacco, snuff and South African sherry are the only products of white civilization which they value. Like the French they recognize nationality by social habits rather than by race. Men and women from other tribes who marry among them and conform to local custom are accepted. In one boma near Arusha I saw a head-man who was by origin a Sikh. I had always thought

Sikhs a remarkably handsome people until I saw him beside the Masai. Those who have been encouraged to seek higher education outside their pastures usually return and at once eagerly readopt the costume and customs of their people. The few who go to the cities are said to turn criminal. Thirty years ago it was predicted that the Masai would become extinct. In fact they have slightly increased in numbers.

March 2nd. The excursion to the Masai was not quite as exhilarating as I had hoped. Early on the cold grey morning the Acting Provincial Commissioner called with the news that the officer who had volunteered to accompany me had gone sick. 'But you'll be all right,' he said, 'your driver knows where to go. You will find the District Commissioner Peebles in camp there and he will show you everything. The place is called Tinka-Tinka. Better take sandwiches with you.'

He presented a police driver to me and addressed him in Swahili; the words 'Tinka-Tinka' occurred in the introduction. The man, who came from Tanga, repeated 'Tinka-Tinka' in a knowledgeable way. It was arranged that he should return in a Landrover after I had breakfasted.

I secured a packet of food and by 9 I and my monoglot driver were on the road, the main road north to Nairobi. We drove for two hours, passing the police post which marked the Kenya frontier. It struck me as odd that an officer of the Tanganyika service should be presiding in Kenya, but I had no means of communicating my doubts

and was dulled by the blank monotony of the countryside. The sun was now out. At length we turned off the
road and came to a stop at a clearing where there stood
six little tin market stalls. The name of the place was
plainly displayed on a painted board 'NGUTATEK'.

'Tinka-Tinka?' I asked.

'Tinka-Tinka.'

I pointed to the sign board but my guide was not only
monoglot but illiterate. 'Tinka-Tinka,' he said firmly.

'Bwana Peebles?' I asked.

'Bwana Peebles,' he replied. Then he got out of the car
and lay down in the shade of a tree.

Great clouds of flies and bees surrounded the little
shops. They were kept by Africans and were stocked
with identical, miscellaneous goods. I entered one and
asked 'Ngutatek?'

'Ngutatek,' the shop keeper confirmed.

'No, Tinka-Tinka?'

'Tinka-Tinka.'

'Bwana Peebles?'

An emphatic shake of the head. 'No Bwana Peebles.'

'D.C.?'

'No D.C.'

I went to my supine driver. 'No Bwana Peebles. No
D.C.'

He nodded vigorously. 'Bwana Peebles, D.C. Tinka
Tinka.'

I despaired and returned to the Landrover. Presently
there appeared a small group of unmistakable Masai,
young warriors covered in ochre; their hair plaited and

coated with red; bracelets and necklaces and ear-rings of copper and beads; spears and knobkerries in hand; their ruddy togas falling loose and open to reveal their dyed flanks. They stared at me and the car. I attempted my little catechism about Tinka and Bwana Peebles. They spat (a politeness, I was told later) and sauntered away. They swaggered into the shops and bought nothing. They swaggered on to my driver and stared at him. He got up and moved further away to the shade of another tree, plainly scared of them. An hour passed. Then there appeared a Kikuyu boy. I welcomed, as I little expected to do when I set out, the evidence in shorts and shirt of European influence. He had a few words of English.

I began my little catechism. No D.C. here. D.C. not coming her. A big meeting of Masai? Not here. Where? That way; pointing vaguely into the bush. But is this Tinka-Tinka. Tinka that way, just here. He pointed to some huts half a mile distant. Show me. I roused my driver. We bumped along the track and found a well with a mechanical pump. This was Tinka. There was no one about. 'Tell this boy in Swahili where the Masai are meeting.' Some conversation ensued, after which my driver got into the car and drove off very crossly in the opposite direction to the one indicated. We drove another twenty miles into Kenya and came to an Indian shop. Here the driver made some enquiries as the result of which he turned the car round and drove furiously back over the road we had travelled.

'Arusha?' I asked.

'Arusha.'

At a river-crossing near the Tanganyika border we had passed an agreeable looking little road-house. Here I made him stop. I did not want to accept defeat without one more effort. The hotelier was English and kindly disposed. Yes, he knew about the Masai gathering, but he thought it was to be a week or two later. He knew where the D.C. was in camp. He explained the mystery of Tinka. It is an onomatopeic word used in those parts for any mechanical device. The pump at the well was a Tinka. There were Tinkas all over the place, one at the site of the D.C.'s camp, which was below the western slopes of Kilimanjaro. The hotelier came out to my driver and explained to him in great detail how to get there. The man repeated the route sullenly but apparently with accuracy. All now seemed set fair. I parted from my rescuer with warm thanks at 1 o'clock. I ate my luncheon which the driver refused to share, whether from religious scruples or sheer bad temper I do not know. We stopped and refilled with petrol at the frontier post. Presently we left the main road and took to dirt tracks. Then it came on to rain.

We were now, it was plain from the quality of the cattle, in an area of European occupation. It seemed an improbable venue for Masai initiation ceremonies. We passed various signs illegible to my driver which indicated farms and government establishments, but he drove on through the mud and rain as fast as he could go with a grim lack of curiosity which suggested confidence. He was following instructions, I assumed. It was three hours before I realized he was completely lost. Then I said

'Arusha', and we were looking for a place to turn in the deep lane when there appeared on foot two uniformed Askaris. These were men from the camp we were seeking. They climbed into the car, directed us and at last, with an hour of daylight left, I met Bwana Peebles, who had expected me at 10 o'clock that morning and now greeted me with good humour.

There was no assembly of the Masai, such as I had been led to expect. That, as the hotelier had said, was in the future. The holy hill where the initiation had to take place was separated from the main tribal grazing grounds by the European farms and it was to arrange a corridor through which the assembly and its herds could pass that the D.C. and his vet were now in camp. The holiness of the hill was traditional; the Masai resolutely maintained their rights to its use, despite any inconvenience to the 'immigrant races', but I gathered the initiation ceremony would be convivial rather than devotional. A warrior may not marry, but he enjoys wide privileges among the unmarried girls of the tribe. When he becomes an elder, he marries, his wife's head is shaven to make her unattractive and an operation is performed which is thought to make her impervious to the temptations of love. His diet is reduced, but his influence in conference grows. It was this transition, in early middle age, that was being prepared at this new Tinka. Half a dozen of the prospective candidates for maturity were there, living in a neighbouring boma. I was invited to enter this little enclosure, where each family has its own hut and its own entrance to the thorn stockade, and the cattle are penned at night among the surrounding dwellings. Cow dung was the main constituent of the architecture.

'If only people would realize that the Masai are just men with two legs,' said the D.C. 'Europeans go quite dotty about them one way or another.'

'Doesn't everyone love them?'

'No, indeed.'

As we were talking a neighbouring farmer, of Boer extraction, came into camp. It was plain that he for one did not at all relish the passage of the Masai through his property. Mr Peebles disabused me of many popular fallacies, such as that the Masai bleed their cattle and subsist on their blood as a staple diet. It is only done, he told me, either ceremoniously or to stop them straying in time of drought. Also of the belief that they are totally untouched by the modern world. When he first came to the district, he told me, before he had learned the language, he was confronted in his office by a Masai warrior in full rig, standing on one leg. He turned to his clerk and said in Swahili: 'Can you find someone to interpret?'

'That will not be necessary,' said the Masai in English. 'I have come to ask for a passport to attend a Boy Scouts' Jamboree in London.'

The rain had passed. Under a watery sunset my dull driver, who had refused food from the Askaris also (I suppose he simply lacked appetite), was given instructions for his return journey which he successfully followed.

I found R. and the brigadier weary from a long day spent wrestling with the problems of government employees.

They have no direct connexion with native administration. At the places we visited on this tour their concern is to resolve the reactions which inevitably occur in isolated communities.

The British officials in Tanganyika are of three groups, none wholly sympathetic to one another. Near the top are those who were young men of military age in 1938 and 1939. They considered at that time that they could best serve their country at a great distance from the European war which all foresaw. These are now in many cases being appointed to Provincial Commissionerships, enjoying seniority to men of their own age who came to Africa after serving, often with distinction, in the armed forces. This second group, now District Commissioners, are inclined to resent this precedence. Below them are the young men who have been produced by the Butler Education Act. These fear that before they can rise very high in the Colonial Service their jobs will be taken by natives. Nor are they all entirely happy in their immediate circumstances. The State, it seems, has not inculcated middle-class prudence in the newly created middle class. In the early days of the British Empire young men without private means did not aspire to support white consorts until they had risen above the lowest ranks. Disease made promotion rapid. The young men coming out from England now come from families in which, traditionally, men marry young. They sadly present budgets which prove that they cannot afford wives, children, motor-cars and the club bar. It is R.'s task to explain that they have no very bitter grievance.

March 3rd. Our next stage was a short one, less than sixty miles to Moshi, the capital of the Chagga country which I had entered from the other side in my trip from Mombasa. It was downhill into a hot plain. I hoped to persuade R. and the brigadier to spend the night at the German hotel on the other side of Kilimanjaro where I had been so comfortable, but there is a huge, brand-new hotel in Moshi itself, built, owned and managed by a Greek; it is named The Livingstone, though Livingstone never came within 200 miles of it. It is the most up to date in Tanganyika, all concrete and plastic and chromium plate, and has proved very useful to film companies who come to make dramas of African life 'on location'. A film company was in occupation of the greater part of it at that moment and their lure proved irresistible to the brigadier, who hoped to find a galaxy of Hollywood starlets. In this he was disappointed. The heroines had already done their part and packed up, leaving the hero, of international repute, and a large, exclusively male rear column of cameramen and 'executives'. But The Livingstone was well equipped and well served, like a liner unaccountably stranded.

Let me here give a word of advice to fellow-tourists in East Africa: keep away from hotels run by the British. We have no calling to this profession. Things are often better further south, but in Tanganyika especially all the defects which distress us at home are accentuated. The forbidding young women who stand behind the 'reception' counters in English provincial hotels have taken the place of post office clerks in the popular imagination for their combination of aloofness with incompetence. Many a weary traveller must have wondered what these wretches do in their hours of leisure. In East Africa he can find out. They sit about with their patrons and make bright conversation. We had suffered from them already and I was to suffer more. Nothing like that happened at the Livingstone. But I felt homesick for the cool verandah of Kibo.

Arusha is a colonial town. Moshi is a model of what liberals hope to see in a self-governing dominion. The Chagga number about 300,000; their land is fertile and healthy. They have in recent years evolved something like a constitutional monarchy. When the Germans came they found a number of local chiefs divided by rivalries which sometimes became violent. They hanged a number of chiefs and appointed one Marealle as paramount. It is his grandson who now reigns as Mshumbree Marealle II, the Mangi Mkuu. He is not infrequently spoken of as 'King Tom'. Under him sits the Chagga Council comprising 3 Divisional Chiefs, 17 Area Chiefs, 17 elected members, 6 nominated and 6 co-opted members. There is an independent judicature. By all accounts it works well and the Chagga have ambitions of absorbing their neighbours, the Pare.

We arrived at Moshi at 9 o'clock in the morning. The brigadier's eyes brightly scanned the hall of the hotel but was told that the film company had already set out for their day's work. They had hired a number of corner-boys and were dressing them up as Masai and teaching them 'tribal' dances.

I was taken off to the Council Offices and introduced to the paramount chief. The Council Offices are brand-new, spic and span, all paid for from local revenue. Marealle is a very engaging young man, who has qualified himself for his high office by taking courses in Social Administration, Economics, Sociology and Psychology at the London School of Economics, without suffering from any of the radical influences popularly associated with that institution. He has also served in Tanganyika as a Welfare Officer and Programmes Manager of the Tanganyika Broadcasting Station and has translated Kipling's 'If' into Kiswahili. He put me in charge of a subordinate to be shown the beauties of his offices and dismissed me with an invitation to dinner that evening, saying: 'Don't trouble to dress. Come in your tatters and rags.'

I am not much of a connoisseur of social and political progress. Another pen than mine is needed to do justice to the really remarkable achievements of the Chagga government. From the Council building I was taken to the KNCU, the Headquarters of the Coffee Co-operative which is the source of almost all the local prosperity. Missionaries introduced the coffee-bean to the slopes of Kilimanjaro and found that it thrived on their property. Dundas, the first British D.C., persuaded the peasants to grow it. Mr Bennett, an Englishman who has spent most of his life in the district, organized the 'co-operative'. Now it is effectively in Chagga hands. I have 'KNCU' plainly written in my diary. What do these initials stand for? I wish I could remember. Presumably something

Chagga or Co-operative Union. Anyway it is a very capacious building in 'contemporary' style. Besides the offices used for the coffee trade it has a shopping arcade, a roof café, a library, bedrooms and a Commercial School, the only one (I think) in Tanganyika. Here I found a mixed class of male and female, Chagga and Indian (male Chaggas predominating), taking a secretarial course. I should have known better than to put my head into that classroom. I have been caught before in this way by nuns. I smirked and attempted to get away when I heard the fateful words '. . . would so much appreciate it if you gave them a little address'.

'I am awfully sorry I haven't anything prepared. There's nothing I could possibly talk about except to say how much I admire everything.'

'Mr Waugh, these boys are all wishing to write good English. Tell them how you learned to write so well.'

Like a P. G. Wodehouse hero I gazed desperately at the rows of dark, curious faces.

'Mr Waugh is a great writer from England. He will tell you how to be great writers.'

'Well,' I said, 'well. I have spent fifty-four years trying to learn English and I still find I have recourse to the dictionary almost every day. English,' I said, warming a little to my subject, 'is incomparably the richest language in the world. There are two or three quite distinct words to express every concept and each has a subtle difference of nuance.'

This was clearly not quite what was required. Consternation was plainly written on all the faces of the aspiring clerks who had greeted me with so broad a welcome.

'What Mr Waugh means,' said the teacher, 'is that English is very simple really. You will not learn all the words. You can make your meaning clear if you know a few of them.'

The students brightened a little. I left it at that.

Dinner that evening was highly enjoyable. R., the brigadier and an English accountant and his newly arrived wife and an elderly Greek doctor and his wife comprised the party. Marealle was in anything but 'tatters and rags'; a dandy with great social grace. His house not fifty miles from the nearest Masai bomas, is of a date with everything in Moshi, entirely European in design and furniture; tiled bathrooms with towels to match their pastel tints, a radiogram in every room, the latest illus-trated papers from England and the U.S.A., a grog tray on the verandah. Only the cooking was African, two delicious curries. I cajoled the accountant's wife into asking our host to turn off the wireless.

Marealle talked with humour of his experiences abroad; of how he had seen people in England eat lobsters, which struck him as peculiarly obscene. 'In Africa,' he said, 'we do not like to eat small things.' He had been sent on a tour of the U.S.A., had addressed meetings of Rotarians and made an enormous collection of neck-ties, which after dinner he displayed, all hanging in a specially con-structed cabinet. He is Lutheran by religion, but no bigot; of his brothers, both of whom hold high positions, one is Catholic and the other Mohammedan. 'It simply depends what school you have been to,' he explained. His son, who has spent much of his childhood in Wales, is now at the school at Tabora which I visited when I first passed through the territory. It was new then and regarded rather quizzically as an attempt, unlikely to succeed, to introduce the English Public School system to Africa. Marealle is as hostile to Makerere (the native university in Uganda) as any die-hard colonial. Outside England I have never heard a good word for Makerere.

After dinner, when we had fully appreciated the ties, we saw the album of souvenirs of his visit to the Queen's Coronation.

We sat on the verandah. Glasses were refilled. The wireless was on. In almost every official utterance homage is paid to the idea of 'the Tanganyikan advance in nationhood'. For someone as unpolitical as myself it is difficult to guess what is meant by 'a nation' of peoples as dissimilar as the Chagga, the Masai, the Gogo, the Arabs of Pagani, the fishermen of Kilwa, the Greek and Indian magnates of Dar-es-Salaam, whose frontiers were arbitrarily drawn in Europe by politicians who had never set foot in Africa.

March 4th. Early this morning we caught our only glimpse of the film company. As the brigadier and I stood in the hall settling our bills there swept past us a handsome man surrounded by understrappers. One of the understrappers picked up the brigadier's attaché case and followed the hero. Too quick for pursuit, the party climbed into their cars and drove off to the game reserve beyond the reach of any communication. The brigadier's case contained the confidential reports on the entire secretariat of the district. He accepted the loss in a soldierly fashion as part of the fortunes of war. When I said good-bye to him eight days later in Dar, he had still had no news of his lost property.

We drove south to Same, where R. had business, lunched with the D.C. in the Pare country. Here the talk was once more of witchcraft. We were out of the country of constitutional monarchy and co-operative prosperity.

That evening we celebrated R.'s forty-fifth birthday in an enchanting rickety little German-kept hotel at Soni, perched above a waterfall on the hill leading to Lushoto, where the Germans had a summer residency, a large garrison and many tea planters. The British governor has a pleasant house there, but he conscientiously sits out the hot season in Dar and lends the place to invalids.

March 5th. We hoped to drive over the hills to Koragwe, but the road was impassable, so we took the low, main road. At Koragwe we are back in sisal country. The D.C. gave a morning party to his highly cosmopolitan neighbours, a Pole, two Parsees, a man from Natal, a Dutchman, a Swahili mayor and an Irishman late of the Palestine Police. He suffers none of the isolation among officials which saddened the life of Same. We came into the hot belt of Tanga.

March 6th. I have already described the chief pleasure of Tanga – the trip to Pangani. I was also shown a municipal beer hall, the George VI Memorial Library, the German built government offices. The sisal trade is the paramount concern of the town.

I paid a call on one of the relics of German colonization, a handsome elderly junker and his wife living in a saw mill they had built for themselves in the bush. Coats-of-arms and hunting trophies hung round the cabin. His father was an early settler, arriving in the 1880s and being granted huge estates in the Lushoto area and elsewhere. These were confiscated in the first World War in which my host's father fell, serving under von Letow. The family still had estates in Germany but my host returned to Tanganyika, watched the decay of the German system, hoped for the restoration of the territory to Germany, was arrested in 1939 and spent the war in a prison camp. He waits resignedly to see the administration surrendered to the natives. He is not very prosperous now. He does not expect to prosper by the change of government. He makes hard wood blocks for parquet floors, which, he remarks, are of too high quality for the modern market. His grandfather to practise himself in arms had taken a commission in the British army and had fallen at Sebastopol. He spoke with pride of his brother who was one of those Prussians who ensured the integrity of the military tradition by going, after 1918, to train the Russian army. What had become of him? Oh, he had fallen at Sebastopol too in the last war, fighting the soldiers whom he had helped train, who confiscated the estates in Prussia and Saxony. He saw no irony in this fate; merely the fulfilment of his family's warlike vocation. There was no element of self-pity or of self-doubt in this much dis-possessed person.

March 7th. A swift uneventful drive back to Dar-es-Salaam, some 350 miles through Koragwe and Moro-goro once more, as the coast road is impassable.

March 8th, 9th, 10th, 11th. Peaceful empty days and sociable evenings. I found in the Club library several books I missed when they were first published, among them *Black Lamb and Grey Falcon* by Dame Rebecca West. I notice she repeatedly describes the Croats (in whose affairs I once played a minute and ignoble part) as 'angry young men'. Did she, I wonder, coin the phrase?

The English newspapers, which reached us four days late, reported great excitement about disturbances in Nyasaland. The ladies who worked as cypher-clerks in Government House were sometimes called away in the middle of dinner to deal with incoming despatches. This was the full extent of the 'emergency' as far as I saw it. A socialist Member of Parliament spent some days in the town, in transit. He had been evicted from somewhere, but whether from Nyasaland, Northern Rhodesia or Southern Rhodesia no one seemed to know. I asked what he had said of an inflammatory nature, where, to whom and in what language, but got no answer until eventually *The Times* appeared on the Club table. There was then no noticeable rush of members to inform themselves. A good deal more interest was taken in the outcome of a case then being heard in which the widow of a local Greek magnate was contesting his will. Q.C.s had been flown out from England to argue the matter. Their presence caused more remark than the politician's.

Tourist traffic to Nyasaland was interrupted. I therefore decided to leave across the frontier of Northern Rhodesia.

March 12*th*.   R. drove me on my way as far as Iringa in the southern highlands. We started at dawn and arrived in time for a late luncheon being delayed for half an hour by an elephant who stepped into the road 200 yards ahead of us. We stopped. He stood facing us, twitching his ears – a sign, I am told, of vexation. Elephants have been known to charge cars. He was very large, with fine tusks. R.s fear for his Mercedes-Benz was controlled but acute. He turned and drove back quarter of a mile. 'I *think* we can go faster than he can over a long distance,' he said. Then we waited until in his own time the elephant ambled away into the bush.

Iringa is a cool, pleasant little town with a railway station but no railway and an excellent Greek restaurant. The natives of the place are called, if I heard aright, 'Hehe', a warlike people who defeated a German column and hold themselves superior to the Masai. When the Masai last invaded, the grandfather of the present chief contemptuously put his sister in command of his forces. She drove them back with great slaughter. Now they mostly go to work in the copper mines and return dressed as cinema cowboys. There were many of them swaggering about the streets with spurs, ornamented leather work, brilliant shirts, huge hats; but most of the inhabitants of the town are Greek and Indian.

There was some jubilation that day in honour of a posse of police who had returned from pacifying Fort Hill across the Nyasa border; one of the few places where the disturbances had seemed formidable.

Here we were joined by Mr Newman, the D.C. from Mbeya, some 150 miles south-west, the place from which I was to take the aeroplane to Rhodesia. Mr Newman is a stalwart ex-airman whose post lies nearest to Nyasa of any in Tanganyika. He was serenely unimpressed by the rumours of danger which had been brought by some Indian refugees from the disturbed area.

There is a current explanation of the reports that European cars are being stoned. The responsible Ministry in Rhodesia is said to have instituted an investigation into traffic. Since the native observers are not handy with paper and pencil, they were instructed to put a stone into a basket for every vehicle that passed them. A journalist finding a man at the side of the road with a basketful of stones asked what they were for and received the answer. 'For cars.'

March 31*th.* I said good-bye to R. and his Mercedes-Benz and drove on with Mr Newman in his Landrover. It is tedious to the reader to be presented with long expressions of gratitude for the kindnesses an author receives in his travels. It must already be abundantly clear that R. had devised nearly all the pleasures of the last weeks. Mr Newman took me from him and for the next two days did all that the oldest friend could have done for the stranger thrust upon him.

The road climbs from Iringa to Mbeya; at the end one is chilly and breathless. We stopped briefly at the Consolata Father's mission, a fine group of buildings like a small Italian town. 'They are the most powerful people in the district,' said Mr Newman. With the sinking of heart always accompanying the inspection of school laboratories, I was shown the thriving schools. Then the old priest who was guiding us, an Italian long habituated to Africa, spoke of African 'nationalism'. The mistake, he said, was to introduce 'Africanization' through politics instead of through service. None of the young men now filling the lower government offices should have been sent from England. Natives should have filled those places and an all-African administration should have been built up from the bottom. Instead we contemplated handing over the highest posts to men who had nothing except the ability to make themselves popular. Like everyone I met he spoke well of Mr Nyerere, but he doubted the ability of his party to govern.

It was not a new point of view, but the speaker gave it authority. British officials say that you cannot leave a native Field Officer in charge of a road-gang. He either cheats them or the government, favours his own tribe or kin, lacks authority and so on. (In fact, in Tanganyika a large number of foremen are half-breeds from the Seychelles, who are found to be more skilful than natives in what used to be called 'man-management'.) It is the debate that occupies all the colonial territories, in which a stranger would be absurd to join. What does seem plain to me is that if the Groundnuts Scheme had been conceived and executed by natives, everyone would point to it as incontrovertible evidence that they were unfit to manage their own affairs.

We came into open downland where the pasture, I was told, is not as good as it looks. Here, in the Sao hills, in a climate rather like that of Kenya, there subsists a little pocket of settlers who live rather as my old friends used to live in the 'Happy Valley'. If I was told the truth, they are rather more bizarre. One of them has turned Moham-medan; another came to a tea-party given for Princess Margaret with his own teapot full of brandy and ginger ale. There is a field for research here, I was told, in that sparse grassland, under that kinetic glare, in that absence of atmosphere, for Kinsey and Wolfenden. I should have liked to linger, but we drove on. In the next range of hills Mr Newman had lately been busy arresting and rusticat-ing a school of witches whose fertility cult required human blood-letting on a scale which often proved fatal. We reached Mr Newman's house at tea-time.

Mbeya is a little English garden-suburb with no par-ticular reason for existence. It was built in the 1930s as a Provincial capital at the time when gold was mined there. Now there is a little aerodrome and a collection of red roofs among conifers and eucalyptus trees, a bank, a post office, a police station. There is also an hotel, named after the non-existent railway, where at that time, it was re-puted, there lurked some disgruntled English journalists who had been forbidden entrance to Nyasaland; they were now engaged in causing annoyance among the reserved and isolated community by interviewing the

Indians and American missionaries who had taken alarm and sought refuge here. Mrs Newman forbade me to go to this hotel and very kindly put me up for the night in her own cheerful villa. That evening she collected some of her neighbours for cocktails. All were officials; all on easy, intimate terms with one another. One of the D.O.s kept guinea-pigs; a doctor had a very numerous family; the P.C. was Australian. All were most welcoming to a rather travel-worn stranger.

March 14*th*.   Rain. I was taken to the police station to have my passport stamped, to the bank, to the office of the airline and to the club, where I again met the policeman, the banker, the official of the air line; also the guests of the evening before; the disgruntled journalists were not among those present.

There was a long wait at the aerodrome. The building consisted of a neat little waiting-room with a good deal of window on which the rain beat hard. It was pleasant to find a place dedicated to this form of travel which lacked a loud-speaker, but it was none the less a drab and depressing spot. Large docks in recent years have become mere tunnels through which one passes from ship to train, but the delights of the water-front of small ports, everywhere in the world, are still unspoiled. Small aerodromes have nothing to offer except shelter and boredom. Presently there was a noise in the sky and the vehicle appeared through the rain. We were off by 3.30 and bumped about above the clouds, seeing nothing.

6 · The Rhodesias

The civilized route to Southern Rhodesia is from Beira in
Portuguese East Africa. That is the way Cecil Rhodes
came when he visited and scolded the disgruntled body
of pioneers who had toiled up from the south. He coveted
Beira, which he saw as the natural opening to the new
territories, and tried to pick a quarrel with the Portuguese.
Lord Salisbury refused to go to war on his behalf. Beira
remains Portuguese, and air-conditioned sleepers now
carry the wise travellers out of the hot coast to the frontier
near Umtali. But, alas, I have never travelled on this route.
I have come by train from Elizabethville and by air from
London. Now I was committed to a very uncomfortable
little vehicle. Had I wished I could have gone straight
through to Salisbury, but this would have caused me to
arrive at a later hour than was convenient for my hosts,
who live some forty miles out. Accordingly I arranged to
spend the night at Ndola, in Northern Rhodesia, near the
Belgian frontier. As soon as it was impossible to write
legibly we were presented with the usual sheaf of official
forms to fill. Could they not have been provided during

our hour-long vigil in the hut which at least provided chairs and a table?

I say 'the usual official forms', but one was unique in my experience. In order to spend one night in transit at Ndola I was required, among other things, to inform the Federal authorities of the names, ages, sexes, dates and places of birth of children *not* accompanying me (six in my case, whose birthdays I can never remember; they remind me in good time), date and place of marriage. What European languages could I write? The oddest demand was to state 'sex of wife'. No question was asked about 'sex of husband'. A note explained: 'All information asked for is necessary to either comply with the law or for statistical purpose'.

An argumentative man might, I suppose, have refused information which did not comply with the law. I filled it all in obediently in a hand-writing, shaken by the machine, which must I fear be causing over-work to the statisticians at Ndola.

'That fellow who stayed here on 14th March – what do you make the name of the eldest son who didn't accompany him – Might be Audubon?'

'Or Anderson.'

'Pass it to the Department of Epigraphy at Lusaka.'

'Or Salisbury.'

'They will pass it on to Salisbury.'

'At least we've got his birthday.'

'Yes, that's the great thing.'

'But the Immigration Office have no business to let him through leaving an ambiguity of this kind.'

'Not enough men for the job.'

'We ought to increase the establishment.'

'We will.'

Looking at the form again (I kept a copy as a souvenir) I see I was too conscientious. Visitors for periods of less than sixty days need not answer questions 13 to 18. So I need not have affirmed pretentions to write English. Rhodesians have good reason to be suspicious of English journalists, but it is, surely, naïve to suppose that it takes sixty days to compose an article traducing them.

Nor need I have stated that I was free from infectious or communicable diseases. That seems odder still, for it is one of the few sane questions. No country welcomes the plague-stricken. In fifty-nine days an active carrier should be able to broadcast his diseases liberally.

Here fully displayed are the arts of modern government for which, it is popularly believed, the native races are not yet far enough advanced.

For the last hour of the flight there was no cloud and we could see a huge expanse of apparently quite empty country; lake, swamp, bush, no sign of a road or village. The apparent emptiness of Africa seems to belie the popular claims to land-hunger, but no doubt there are good reasons for it which the tourist does not understand.

The sun set and we came in by darkness.

The agent of the statisticians was civil enough. A room had been booked for me in the town. There was a bus to take me there. I was the only transit-passenger.

Ndola is south-east of Mbeya, on the railway which joins the Congo to Cape Town. I passed through it many years ago in a train. We arrived at 7.15 by my watch; 6.15 by local time. The town has grown beyond recognition and is growing fast, spreading itself in the manner of modern Africa, where land is cheap and everybody worth the planners' consideration has a motor-car, along broad boulevards in a litter of concrete. The hotel alone, one-storied, stucco-faced, soon no doubt to be demolished and rebuilt, is a relic of pioneer days. The builders had plainly some faint memories of the column and architrave. Everything else in sight was 'contemporary'.

It was a hot, airless evening heavy with the fumes of metallurgy. The real copper-belt where white artisans, it is said, live the life of an American country club and honoured guests are luxuriously feasted, lies at some distance. Ndola, like every part of the continent, is in transition. It is already purely a white man's town. On this Saturday evening there were fewer Africans in the streets than would be seen in London. Most of the white men seemed to be drunk.

I left my bags in a sad little, stuffy bedroom, lit by a single faintly glowing bulb, and I wandered out. Attracted by a neon sign which read: 'TAVERN. OLD ENGLISH ATMOSPHERE', I descended concrete steps to a basement-bar, softly lit and pervaded by 'background music'. The barman was white and wore his hair in the Teddy-boy style. A white lady, whom I took to be a tart, sat before him. She had an odd look of Mrs Stitch. Four or five youngish Rhodesians were drinking with her. The old English atmosphere was provided by chair and tables made to look rather like beer barrels.

The bar of the hotel, to which I adjourned, was more congenial. I had no appetite for dinner and asked for some sandwiches. When they were brought, a frightfully drunk man came and devoured most of them. He was, he told me, a philosopher who had lost his soul.

'He's a nice enough fellow,' said the barman, 'except on Saturday nights.'

While he ate my sandwiches he uttered a great deal of vaguely familiar English verse. I think he was just stringing together as many odd lines of Shakespeare and Macaulay and Wordsworth and Kipling as had remained in his mind from some not very remote period of schooling; he improvising a little in part poetic, part Biblical style on the subject of his own evident unpopularity.

A much less drunk man came to protect me.

'You mustn't mind him. He's a bloody nuisance.'

This new friend was stout and affable. I should have taken him for a military man had he not assured me he had served in the Navy and the Air Force. He later confirmed my first speculation by claiming to having been in the Black Watch. He also said he was Irish.

The philosopher then said: 'Don't believe him, he's not Scotch. He only says he is because he went to Fettes.'

Suddenly, apropos of nothing, the barman said :'D'you happen to know Ed Stanley of Alderley?'

By what mannerism or turn of phrase had I betrayed this arcane knowledge? Perhaps it was the barman's habitual gambit to all visiting Englishmen.

'Sheffield to me,' I replied.

'I am a great friend of his lordship,' said the barman.

He then recited the names of some dozen noblemen of his acquaintance. I could join him in one or two cases. This did not endear him to the philosopher, who had formed a low view of aristocracy without, he was at pains to assure me, indulging any respect for democracy.

My stout champion said wistfully: 'I left all that sort of thing behind when I came out here.'

The barman, however, was so pleased that he fetched the manageress to see me.

'A friend of Lord Stanley of Alderley's.'

'Sheffield's. You know him? He has been here?'

'No, I'm afraid I've never heard of him. I hope you'll be comfortable here. What room have they given you?' I told her. 'Oh, dear, that won't do, will it? I'll have your things moved.'

So when, very early, I escaped from my companions I found myself quartered in a fine suite — sitting-room, bedroom, bright lights, flowing water, where I lay very contented while the sounds of a Ndola Saturday night waxed and raged about me until, before dawn, I slipped out to the aerodrome bus in the now silent street.

15th March. The aeroplane from Ndola was rather more comfortable than the machine that brought me from Mbeya and the portholes afforded glimpses of a less desolate terrain than the swamps of Northern Rhodesia. About half-way through the flight we crossed the border of Southern Rhodesia. As we approached Salisbury we might have been over Surrey. Distance gives a trimness, which I knew from previous experience is largely illusory, to the great commercial suburb which has flooded over Matabeleland and Mashonaland.

The friends I was coming to visit are named John and Daphne. Neither was at the aerodrome to meet me; nor at the office in the city. A telephone call, made through an instrument of novel design, which concealed its dial under its base, disclosed that I was not expected until next week. But with imperturbable goodwill Daphne said she would come for me at once.

I had an hour to wait.

Salisbury is changing dizzily. The airline headquarters where I stood was brand-new since last year. Next to it Meikle's Hotel, which on my last visit had some architectural affinities with the hotel at Ndola, had sprung up into a slightly smaller version of the Rockefeller Center in New York. Behind it a tower, slightly lower than the Empire State Building, crowned by a sphere (luminous and opalescent in the hours of darkness), has arisen to accommodate an insurance company. On this Sunday morning the broad streets were empty. The trees were just shedding their flowers. The air was fresh, the sun brilliant and pleasantly warm. At length Daphne arrived and bore me off to Mazoe, near which she and her huge family have been settled for ten years.

John's fortunes are typical of the new Rhodesia. He returned to England from the army in 1945 eager to work and develop his ancestral estates, found himself frustrated by official regulations, impetuously bought an agricultural property, unseen, forty miles out of Salisbury, and removed there with his wife, children and family portraits and much of his livestock. The estate is very large by English standards, but of moderate, viable size for Africa. There was no Labour Government there to vex him, no elaborate regulations or oppressive taxation, but Africa imposes its own discouragements. The farm does not pay its way. He is now a prosperous business-man driving daily to an office in the city as though to London from Sunningdale, preserving a strong link with his former way of life through his racing stable. He is a director of a bank and several commercial enterprises. His main activity is to manufacture paper bags out of imported materials. His sons go to school in Salisbury and speak in a different accent from their parents, the girls to convents in Umtali and South Africa. They go for seaside holidays to Durban. None of them have any sentimental yearnings for their homeland.

The house is a long bungalow stretching across the hillside, roofed with iron, walled with concrete, making no claim to architectural character. A short distance away is the 'native compound', the village of round huts from which sounds of revelry can often be heard long into the night. All John's labour, house-boys and farm boys alike, come from Nyasaland. He has built them a school and employs an African teacher and an English chaplain. Many have become Christians.

After the great plantation of fruit and the reservoir which are the chief surviving achievements in this area of the old Charter Company, the road becomes rougher. There is a road-house which was once a stage-post in the days of travel by horse and coach. It has now developed a swimming-pool and café tables. Soon after it we turn into John's drive, a steep earth track. White teeth flash and pink palms flutter in greeting as we pass the groups and couples of Nyasas. Then we stop at the house and emerge into dust or mud according to the season.

Today, Sunday, there are no gardeners at work; usually they can be found deep in weed languidly lopping it with tools like golf-clubs. This morning all are on holiday except a small group who are excavating a swimming-pool. They are in a frenzy of righteous activity for they belong to a peculiar half-Christian sect which holds it to be immoral to rest on Sundays.

The house is always thronged but never, apparently, full. My hostess serenely welcomes all comers, friends from England, neighbours, business associates of her husband, relations; but children predominate. The verandah, here called a 'stoep', is their playground. African nurses are not employed much in Rhodesia. There is no nursery. There is a school-room imposingly furnished with desks, black board and terrestrial globe, but it never contains its children for more than a few minutes at a time. Tricycle riding round the stoep is the favourite pastime.

It is not a restful house by any ordinary standard, but Daphne's personality mysteriously imposes a kind of overriding peace above the turmoil.

16th March. Though I have taken advantage of every comfort Africa affords, I am travel-worn. I have covered a lot of ground one way and another and am glad of a day's inactivity – it cannot be called repose. The teeming life of the house, as in a back-street of Naples, rages round me from dawn to dusk, but I remain in my chair, subject to interrogation, and the performances of conjuring, dancing and exhibitions of strength, but for one day at least immovable.

17th March. We set out in a party of four – Daphne, her chaplain and a kind young manufacturer of paper bags – to drive to the Eastern Highlands.

First we spent a few minutes at the tobacco sales, which are a great annual event of Salisbury. The tobacco stands baled in long rows in the great warehouses. The buyers follow the auctioneer in swift procession sampling and bidding as they go. The auctioneer saunters from bale to bale with an illusion of nonchalance. He has been imported at great expense from New Orleans and is master of his odd trade. He croons continuously, and to the layman, quite unintelligibly, sometimes in a monotone, sometimes breaking into popular melody. He is running up the prices and knocking down the lots with a precision all the more impressive for being entirely mysterious. This, they tell me, is how tobacco is bought and sold everywhere in the world. It is wildly unlike Mr E. M. Forster's description in *Pharos and Pharillon* of the cotton market in Alexandria. Prices were rather low that morning, I gathered. The tobacco crop is the only prosperous agricultural undertaking in Southern Rhodesia and there were some long faces, but the farmers' ladies sat in hats, gloves and their best clothes, cheerfully drinking coffee.

Some 160 miles of railway and good road lead from Salisbury to Umtali. This, as I have noted, is the route by which the wise traveller enters the country. The Eastern Highlands march with the Portuguese frontier. They comprise some of the finest natural scenery in Africa, wooded mountains, waterfalls, keen air, an area of special fascination to the ornithologist and ento-mologist; to the archaeologist also, for here are the finely built stone terraces and unexplained dens of Inyanga. An undated civilization once flourished here and today there are for the tourist, to my knowledge, two admirable hotels and, by repute, more.

One, where we lunched – by far the best hotel meal since Malindi – is in the main street of Umtali, the capital and centre of this happy land, a spacious garden-city round which many rich immigrants have built themselves villas and laid out gardens.

The object of our visit was to see Daphne's daughter, Jill, who is at school in a brand-new convent which American nuns, who profess a devotion (unfamiliar to me) to 'the Sacred Heart of Mary', have built in the out-skirts of the town – a sumptuous place with a bathroom to every two girls. It was a little depressing to find American pseudo-anatomical charts illustrating the ill effects of wine on the human body; also to find text-books of local history composed for use in the Union of South Africa. A more modern note was struck by the appear-ance of 'Charm' in the time-table of the curriculum. This,

on investigation, proved to be the new name for Deportment. And very engaging the deportment of the girls was
as they skidded past us in the corridors with little
genuflections.

I tried to buy native artifacts in the shops of Umtali.
Some tribes of Portuguese East Africa carve very well, as
I had seen in the collection made by one of the district
officers at Kilwa. But here, almost on the frontier, there
was nothing for sale except the most trashy tourist
souvenirs. On advice from one shopkeeper we followed
our quest to the native quarter, well built and well kept,
but hardly welcoming. As at a military establishment
there were notices warning-off unauthorized visitors,
summoning new arrivals to medical inspection and regis-
tration. And there were no carvings to be found.

We drove on higher into the mountains, past a riding-
school and the gates of many handsome properties,
through a landscape of stupendous beauty to another
excellent hotel named Leopard's Rock.

I have said that the Eastern Highlands are the proper
approach to Rhodesia. In fact, the holiday-maker need
go no further. A booklet issued by the office of Tourist
Development sets out the attractions of the district with
a moderation which contrasts pleasantly with the language usually employed in such publications. It is
admitted that there is neither snow nor sea, but there is
everything else; in Umtali golf, bowls, lawn tennis, riding,
a camping site (with bathrooms), a theatre, cinemas, a
Rotary Club, a Round Table, Lodges of English and
Scottish Freemasons, and a Catholic Bishop; at Inyanga,

Cecil Rhodes's estate is now a National Park, with a trout-hatchery, a lake for bathing (no bilharzia in the mountain waters) and boating, a camp of log cabins in the Tyrolean style; in the Vumba hills there are pretty Samango monkeys; everywhere there are waterfalls – ferns and great trees – well, there is no need to transcribe the whole official encomium; enough to say that it is true. Charabancs have not yet appeared to despoil the place. It is what the natural beauty spots of Europe must have been sixty years ago.

That evening after dinner we sat before a log fire and went to bed in pretty chintzy rooms surrounded by cool, mountain silence. The bill next morning was not excessive.

I should have liked to linger and go further. I hope to return. Perhaps the development of this district may provide the elderly and well-to-do with a more dignified resort than the beaches where they now exhibit themselves. The craze for sunburn has lasted long enough. On the Riviera the survivors and imitators of the elegant young neurotics of Scott Fitzgerald's *Tender is the Night* have grown into those greasy hulks of flesh which are now being hemmed in and invaded by the proletariat. If fashion is to be true to its metier, it must seek seclusion. Where better than here?

March 18th. A long day's drive; back to Uumtali first, then seventy-six miles due south through the hills, dropping at midday into the hot valley of the Sabi, turning west over Birchenough bridge for some hundred miles of bush and grass country to Zimbabwe, which we reached just before sunset.

I had been here before from Fort Victoria and had fairly thoroughly surveyed these famous ruins – the most remarkable in Africa south of Egypt. Daphne and the others were on their first visit. There was not time that evening to do more than appreciate the general aspect. The rest of the party returned at dawn next day.

There was once a great stone city here of which two main groups of building survive in impressive form. Their aspect has been too often photographed and described to need a detailed account here. Their origin remains a mystery and the ground of acrimonious dispute. They are unique in their size and state of preservation, but there are other 'Zimbabwes' – a word indifferently translated as a 'court' or 'a stone building'. This is correctly called the Great Zimbabwe.

When the first white man came here in 1868 the elliptical enclosure popularly known as the Temple was deserted and densely overgrown. The hilltop called the Acropolis was used by a neighbouring tribe as a cattle kraal and remained in their use for nearly thirty years longer. In the early days of the Charter Company a concession was given to an 'Ancient Ruins Company' formed with a capital of £25,000 to prospect for gold in all the archaeological sites between the Limpopo and the Zambesi. It lasted until 1903. No record survives of its depredations. Doubtless numerous artifacts were unearthed and melted down. The damage done by the excavations is now deeply deplored and recent administrations have been at pains to mitigate it.

At Great Zimbabwe the bush has been cleared. It is admirably kept (part of it, indeed, laid out as a golf links); fallen stones have been replaced, paths and, where necessary, steps laid down. The aspect is of Devon parkland, strewn everywhere with natural boulders, outcrops of rock and lines of masonry.

The Acropolis is a steep little hill some 350 feet high, approached originally only through two narrow clefts in the granite. The custodians have laid out a gentler path, interspersed with seats, for the benefit of elderly visitors. The summit is a mass of fortifications and partitions built among the natural boulders and rock face. It was once, presumably, a place of refuge; also of industry. Gold was smelted here although no gold diggings have been found near it. Many objects of arachaeological value were probably found here by the white pioneers, most of which were destroyed. Of what remains, some are in the museum at Bulawayo, but much was taken to Cape Town in the days when it seemed likely that that city would be the capital of a great British commonwealth country.

The Temple stands more than a quarter of a mile distant. It is a great oval of massive and highly skilfully laid drystone wall surmounted for 265 feet of its length with an ornamental coping of a double strip of chevron pattern. The entrances have been rebuilt, not as they were. Now they are gaps open to the top with rounded sides suggesting Cotswold buttresses. Originally there were doorways each with a beam, and above the beam con-

tinuous wall. The outer wall is sixteen feet thick at the
bottom. The guide-book does not specify its height;
more than twenty feet I should guess. The effect must
have been forbidding. As it stands, many who are sus-
ceptible – Daphne among them – to such impressions
find the place eerie. It is certainly enigmatic. For a large
part of the circumference there is an inner wall as high as
the outer, leaving between them a narrow sunless lane
which leads to a solid conical tower which, of course, has
been dubbed 'phallic'. I am sceptical of these modish
attributions. Are the objects displayed on some of the
new electric railway stations of outer London 'phallic'?
Do they attract a cult? The only explicitly phallic symbol
of recent construction which I know is Wiegland's
obelisk in the suburbs of Oslo. There is no mistaking the
inspiration of that erection. But it lacks worshippers.

Inside the walls the ground shows signs of division;
what was roofed, what was open, what was a ceremonial
court, what a cattle byre, are all conjectural. The appellation 'temple' and the deep shadows have stirred the
imagination to thoughts of bloody and obscene ritual,
but in fact there is no reason for supposing that this was
ever a place of worship. I defy the most ingenious film
director to reconstruct it, and people it at all plausibly
with priests and priestesses. A visitor from Mars to the
Catholic Cathedral in Salisbury, Rhodesia, would recog-
nise that he was in a building made by the same kind of
people (living in a debased age) and for the same purpose
as in Salisbury, England. But 'the Temple' at Zimbabwe
leaves the visitor from Europe without any comparison.

It is an example of what so often moved G. K. Chesterton to revulsion. It is the Wrong Shape. Something utterly alien.

Nor do there seem to be any native traditions of sanctity. The latest excavators are inclined to think it was a royal kraal, that the outer wall is later than the inner, that the conical erection was a watch-tower or simply a grandiose monument to personal splendour. They think it was built fairly recently by Bantus.

Recently, that is to say, in comparison to some of the theories current in Rhodesia. King Solomon, of course, has been proposed as its architect; also an aboriginal and mythical white race, Freemasons to a man; also Indians, Arabs, Persians, even Chinese; anyone but natives; for it is an article of the local faith, held even by the most cultivated Rhodesians, that the Bantu throughout all history has been as they found him sixty years ago, a primitive savage, totally ignorant of the arts of peace. The most they will admit is that possibly black men might have built a stone wall if enslaved and directed by Asiatics. They preferred the theory of the lost white tribe. This was shaken by the results of a 'carbon test' applied to a piece of wood taken from a beam over a drain in the outer wall. There is an electrical appliance, it appears, which can determine the age of wood. Two independent examinations gave the age of this specimen as about 700 years. I don't profess to understand the process. There is, experts say, room for great discrepancy according to whether the specimen is taken from the heart of a tree or from near the surface. The thirteenth-century attribution has been cheerfully welcomed because the Bantus had probably not moved into this region at that time. Bushmen could not have built Zimbabwe. Therefore a non-African race of higher culture did so. Thus runs the popular argument. But one need not be a scientist to question the significance of the test. Many modern villas in the home counties incorporate genuine Tudor beams; many ancient houses have been repaired with new timber. Wood has long been scarce in the region of Zimbabwe. Nothing is more likely than that builders of whatever age or race make use of beams from earlier structures. The 'carbon test' has really added nothing to our knowledge of the date of the masonry.

There is a choice of hotels within easy reach of the ruins. We chose badly. I noted in my diary: 'kept by fiend', which meant that we were back in the grip of those affable British manageresses of whom I have already warned the reader. I will not, from respect for the law of libel, identify the place, nor, from respect for my reader's patience, expatiate on our sufferings.

March 19*th*.   We escaped early and joined the main road that runs from Beit Bridge through Fort Victoria to Salisbury. Fort Victoria has sentimental associations for Rhodesians as the first settlement, established in 1890 by the Pioneer Column as it marched from Bechuanaland into Mashonaland. A little watch-tower survives of the original defences. Now there are shops, a cinema, an hotel, a new civic hall and a fine little Catholic church designed by the architect whose main work we were on our way to visit. Not many people live in the town. It is a market centre for farmers, and ox-waggons can still be seen in the broad streets.

Serima Mission lies off the main road in the native reserve behind a large European estate named Chatsworth. Here again it was my companions' first visit. I had been there a year ago and was eager to show them what seemed to me one of the most remarkable enterprises in the country; also to see what progress had been made in the year and to meet the architect, Fr Groeber, who had been away when I was last there. Serima does not advertise itself or welcome idle sight-seers. It exists for its own people. None of its products is sent out for sale or for exhibition. As far as I know no photographs have ever been published. There are no sign-posts to direct the traveller along the sandy tracks which run through the flat, sparsely grown country.

It is in the diocese of Gwelo, entrusted to the Swiss Bethlehem Fathers. In 1948 Fr Groeber was sent by his bishop to found and design the Mission. The available funds were, and are, pitifully inadequate. Everything was lacking except space and zeal. The staff at present consists of one other priest, a lay brother skilled in building, and six Mary Ward nuns. They have a school of 170 Mashona boarders and, nearing completion, the large and remarkable church which we had come to see.

It is this that one first notices as one emerges from the bush, and at first sight it affords no pleasure to an eye such as mine which is dull to contemporary taste. Geometrical, economical, constructed of concrete and corrugated iron, it rises from the centre of its bleak site like the hangar of a deserted airfield.

Seen on the drawing-board, Serima is a logical and symmetrical plan. Axial roads converge on the church from the surrounding blocks of dormitories, school-rooms, workshops, refectory and dispensary. But at present these roads are scarcely visible tracks and bare feet have traced other straggling paths across the campus. The 'blocks' are at present represented by low sheds. One day it will be laid out and the intervening areas planted and the architect's conception will be manifested to the layman. At present one needs a keen imagination to appreciate the plan.

Fr Groeber works and sleeps in a single cell opening on the little entrance hall of the main building. His book-shelves are filled with books of ascetic theology and modern art in English, German and French. He is an elderly, serene man. When I said I might be writing some-thing about the place, his welcome became slightly clouded, but he did not forbid me to do so and as he began showing me how he worked, he brightened. In youth he studied architecture in Switzerland and on the day after taking his degree went straight to the seminary, volunteered for the African mission and thought it un-likely he would ever be called to exercise his art. In the last twenty years he has built not only for his own order but for the Jesuits, whose seminary for native priests near Salisbury is from his designs. But Serima is his particular creation. It is here that he has founded the little school of art which is one of the most exhilarating places in Africa.

During the last weeks I have taken every chance of searching bazaars and pedlar's wares for examples of African sculpture. The best, as I have said, were at Kilwa and the work of tribes in Portuguese territory, but they, though skilfully cut, were hopelessly lacking in vision and invention. The same archetypes of animal and human form was repeated again and again. I have seen photographs of figures by natives of the Congo and Uganda which might get exhibited in London and Paris; individual enough, but plainly the work of men who had been shown European sculpture. The savage African art of the eighteenth and early nineteenth centuries which delighted the European and American connoisseurs of the 1920s, seems as dead as the civilized art of Europe.

There is a mission at Cyrene with wall paintings by native artists which I have not visited. From photographs it seems that they were shown conventional European pictures and encouraged to translate them into local idiom, rather as the Mexican Indians of the sixteenth and seventeenth century were set to work on models of the Spanish Renaissance and Baroque – with agreeably picturesque results, certainly, but without planting a living art, capable of free growth. And the Mexican Indians had a long tradition of many ingenious crafts. The Mashona, among whom Fr Groeber works have never had an artist, nor any craft except the weaving by the women of grass mats in very simple patterns. Fr Groeber has been at pains to keep all European models away from his pupils. He has none of the illusions of the recent past, that every man is a natural artist, but in the boys passing through his hands he has found a few – as many perhaps as would be found passing through an English Public School – who have the genuine aesthetic impulse. At present he has two master-carvers in their mid-twenties and a dozen apprentices in their teens. The sort of carving they produce is symbolic and didactic, like that of the European Middle Ages; entirely novel and entirely African.

Every boy on arrival from his village is told to draw an account of his journey. Many are capable of nothing; some produce pictures not much different from the nursery scrawlings of European children some years their juniors. Those with discernible talent are then taught to control the pencil, the chalk, the pen, the brush; they make abstract symmetrical patterns, they draw 'matchstick' hieroglyphics of figures in action. Perhaps all this is a commonplace of 'progressive' education. I don't know. It was quite new to me. Nothing of the kind happened in the drawing classes of my own youth, which began with copying lithographs of rural scenery and advanced to 'freehand' renderings of still life. Clay modelling is the next stage. The boy's first task is always to make a mask which will 'frighten his little brother'. It is explained to him that it is far easier to make ugly things than beautiful; that, implicitly, the paintings of Mr Francis Bacon are a rudimentary accomplishment which the Mashona boy must outgrow. The highest achievement is to make something lovable, an image of angel or saint, of Our Lady or Our Lord, before which it is easy to pray. Before this stage is approached the use of the chisel is taught and the composition of ornaments that express a moral lesson or a theological tenet. Art is the catechism and prayer in visible form. There is no suggestion of self-expression or of aesthetic emotion; nor of acquiring a marketable skill or titillating national pride at doing as well as the white man.

Wood is scarce and not of good quality. Everything is first sketched in clay and the best of the sculptors show themselves sharply critical, modelling many versions before committing one to the chisel.

The first completed work was the main entrance. Here the concrete walls have been painted in simple geometric designs of ochre and umber – earth colours made from the soil of the district. On either side of the door stand crowned effigies of the Pope and the Queen; not attempted portraits, but direct African statements of the African idea of majesty; not remotely comic, very much more august indeed than most modern European official (and non-official) statuary.

The panels of the door display a series carved in high relief illustrating the rewards and dangers of African life. For the industrious apprentice there are the skills of husbandry, the dignity of teaching, family love, or, highest aim, the priesthood; for the idle apprentice, gambling, drinking, dancing, witch-doctors and Mohammedanism.

No work was going on in the church, which is nearing completion. In plan it is, as Fr Groeber remarked, like a pair of shorts. Two rectangular naves are laid, one corner of each touching, at an angle of about forty-five degrees. The axis of the naves converge on the high altar, which stands in a very large five-sided sanctuary. This plan was evolved from the cruciform with the purpose of setting the altar in the fullest view of the largest congregation. In a first design the arms of the cross were drawn down so as to make a kind of broad arrow. Then the triangular area between the two naves became the Lady chapel, with an altar at its apex, through which one enters. Two side chapels prolong the back wall of the sanctuary. There will be a central tower standing clear behind and (I think) an appended sacristry.

It is a building designed for use, to be seen from the inside. A ceiling of traditional grass-mats supported on a frame of slender beams painted in chevrons of earth colours hides the pitch and harsh material of the roof, which is borne on open parabolic arches of concrete.

The most important carvings at present are the entrance and the Stations of the Cross. The door is panelled like that of the mission house with figures and scenes from the Old and New Testaments, chosen to illustrate theological doctrines. The choice of subject is always Fr Groeber's. The Stations, new since my last visit, are in the round, standing out from the wall on brackets. They are the most ambitious and successful of the works at Serima.

Like everything else they are designed for use. I thought of the Stations at the much advertised chapel at Vence, which Matisse scrawled over a single wall in a manner that inhibits the devotion they should occasion.

In the workshop a rood screen is in preparation; four tall posts, whole tree-trunks, carved from top to bottom with figures, and two equally elaborate cross-beams from which a great crucifix is designed to hang. Sanctuary stools, also, were being carved out of solid drums of timber. Quite soon there will be at Serima one of the most beautiful and original churches of the modern world.

That is the aim of the builder; to make a church, not to found an Art School. The sculptors have been called into existence for the church, not the church for the sculptors.

What will happen when Fr Groeber is no longer there to direct them? They are very much younger than he. Their technical skill will remain ripe for well-intentioned exploitation by collectors and museums. How long can their vision remain uncontaminated by Europe and America? Those eager apprentices I saw today will find that there are larger rewards awaiting them for inferior work. With very little labour they can imitate 'expressionist' or 'abstract' models. Something of the kind, I gather, is happening in parts of the Belgian Congo. In less than a full lifetime one has seen so many promising enterprises come to nothing – for example Walt Disney's cartoon films. It would be absurd presumption to suggest that a tradition has been founded at Serima. But to say that is not to belittle the present achievement. It is the fault of the modern eye to be forever goggling ahead, of the modern mind to concern itself only with 'influences' and 'movements', instead of accepting with gratitude the tangible gifts of the past and present. The artist has no concern with the future. Fr Groeber's achievement has been to make Africans do what none but Africans could have done and what no Africans in this huge region ever did before; to leave a church where they and their descendants can worship, which their descendants will cherish with the pride and awe with which we in Europe survey the edifices of our Middle Ages.

The smiling nuns pressed us to stay for luncheon, but my party had business in Salisbury. Soon we were back on the straight, empty main road. We paused briefly at the restaurant of a little mining town, then on again over the plain, and reached the farm where I was staying, before dark.

7 · The Rhodesias Continued

Salisbury – the Matopos – Rhodes

March 20th. The changes in the city are greater than a first glance revealed. The streets, as all the inhabitants often remind one, are laid out so that a team of oxen could be turned in them. Last year there was no 'traffic problem'. Now parking-meters have sprung up everywhere and the leading grocer has built a 'park' on his roof, approached by a ramp like the Guggenheim Gallery in New York. Customers go down to the shop by lift, make their purchases and collect them at the door when they drive down. There are 'drive-in cinemas'. Every sign of the early settlers is disappearing. Also the word 'settler', which is now held to be opprobrious and politically tendentious.

I have already remarked on the difficulties that face a modern traveller in the kaleidoscopic charges of euphemism. In the old days 'settlers' were proud of their distinction from officials. Now they wish to be called plain 'Rhodesians' fearing that their original name suggests recent and temporary occupation. The oddest manipulation of vocabulary is the one by which a white American is classified as a European and a black American as an 'alien native'. 'Native', surely the most honourable appellation for white or black, is never used of whites, and some blacks resent it. 'Nigger' (except as a term of affection used among niggers) and 'Kaffir' have long been thought offensive. 'Bantu' is held to be inexact by anthropologists. 'African' is clearly too vague for use. I am told that in the U.S.A. one may say 'negro' but not 'negress'. They like to be called 'coloured'. But 'coloured' in most of Africa means mulatto. In my lifetime I have seen 'Anglo-Indian', which I still use to describe my mother's family, come to mean Eurasian. Goanese for some mysterious reason are huffy if they are not called 'Goans'. There is no end to the flood of gentilisms that are eroding the language. Well, I don't suppose any blackamoors, niggers, Kaffirs, natives, Bantu or Africans will read this diary. Some whites may, so I apologize for calling some of them 'settlers', but I don't know how else without periphrasis to describe those nice, pinkish people who have come to settle here.

Very few indeed of these settlers survive or descend from the original invaders of seventy years ago. Those who do are very proud of it and display certificates of the fact, like armorial bearing, in their houses. Not all the 'pioneers' were riff-raff. Missionary stock provides a number of the present leading citizens. But the immigration which has changed the character of the country occurred since 1945. This change is illustrated in an exhibition now being held.

There is a fine new building in Salisbury named the Rhodes National Gallery, the gift of one of these recent immigrants. There are as yet no permanent exhibits and the managers have to exercise ingenuity in filling it. When I was here last year there was a collection of enlarged photographs on view, sent round the world by some American cultural organization. The theme appeared to be connected with human progress and the brotherhood of man. The effect was of being enclosed in the pages of a popular magazine. This year there is something more enterprising, a collection of furniture and *objets d'art* lent by private owners in the Federation. The catalogue emphasized its federal character, but everything (I think) comes from Southern Rhodesia and almost everything has been brought here since 1945.

It is organized and introduced by a youngish bachelor who keeps an antique shop, bubbles with the lore of Mr Betjeman and Mr Osbert Lancaster – he has settled at the moment on William IV as the 'nicest' period – and is himself an outstanding example of the change in character of modern Rhodesians from the pioneers. He chose and arranged the exhibits, as far as possible as 'period rooms', the last of which is a sly comment on the taste of his humbler neighbours – a room furnished with pieces of local manufacture more gruesome than anything to be seen even in the shop-windows of England.

There are four collectors in Rhodesia with rich posses-sions; these have provided the most notable pieces. But there are also single exhibits from many widely dispersed houses. John, for example, had lent the superb embroid-ered train worn by his great-great-grandmother at the christening of the King of Rome.

Not everything would attract interest or even be accepted for sale at Sotheby's. Indeed, from my own Somerset neighbours in a five-mile radius I could assemble a more varied and valuable exhibition than the whole Federation can afford. But the significance of the Salisbury Exhibition is that anything worth showing should be there at all; that it is now possible to illustrate with reasonably good examples almost every period of European taste. The recent settlers have brought their household gods with them. This, much more than the skyscrapers, impresses the tourist with a sense of the depth of European settlement. Also of its humanity; for the new settlers have not adopted the narrow habits of thought of their predecessors.

The commercial growth of Salisbury, its towering banks and insurance offices, its neatly dressed Rotarians, make one forget that it is also the seat of government – of two Governments, indeed, with two parliaments, two prime ministers, a Governor-General and a Governor. John and Daphne and I were commanded to a large dinner-party at Government House for a visiting British Minister. It was a pretty sight when the ladies left the table to see them in their long dresses and long white gloves cluster round the door and curtsey like altar boys to the Governor-General. When they had left I found myself sitting next to a local cultivated bigwig. I attempted something polite about how delightful his country was for a visit. He spoke, as politicians will, of the great progress and potentialities of his country.

I said: 'I think you are a bachelor. I should not care to bring up children here.'

'Why not?' rather sharply scenting politics.

'The accent.'

I think there was a glance of sympathy in his eye. He did not expatiate on the educational advantages, the salubrious climate, the opportunities for enrichment. Instead he talked of his own upbringing in England.

When the Governor-General thinks a party has lasted long enough, he sends an A.D.C. to play a record of the Death Song from 'King Kong'.

March 21st. There was racing this afternoon at Mirandellas. In living memory lions were shot where the racecourse now stands. John had a horse running. Daphne and I left him and his chaplain there and drove off into the native reserve in search of a Jesuit missionary I had known in England. He did not know it then, but it was to be his brother who was sent out as head of the official enquiry into the riots in Nyasaland.

One does not see many Africans in Salisbury; fewer it seemed than in London. There are black porters in the larger shops and the white shop-girls are abominably rude to them. They are also rather rude to their white customer, for they are at pains to demonstrate that under God all white men were created equal. The well-paid plumber who comes out to work in a private house expects to sit down in the dining-room with the family. He has a black, ill-paid assistant who squats outside. Here, as in England, the champions of the colour bar are the classes whose modest skills many negroes can master.

Southern Rhodesia differs historically from, say, Uganda and Nyasaland. Here the whites came as conquerors; there the natives voluntarily put themselves under the protection of the English Crown. The conquest was not a feast of arms to be remembered with pride, but it was an exercise of high chivalry compared with the occupation of Australia, where the settlers regularly put out poisoned food for the aborigines. The tribes which were conquered were, in many cases, themselves recent conquerors. Force of arms had always been recognized in Africa as giving right of possession.

The visitor to Rhodesia sees as little of the natives as a visitor in the United States sees little of the very poor. (But in Rhodesia the natives are proportionately more numerous than the destitute in America.) They have no obvious tribal characteristics. They are not beautiful like the Masai or buoyant like the Wachagga or picturesquely prehistoric like the Wagogo. All wear a drab uniform of shirt and shorts. They have the hang-dog air of the defeated people, which indeed they are.

Colonel David Stirling, with whom I served in the war, came here on a commercial enterprise and was so depressed by the conditions of the natives that he has devoted the last ten years of his life to persuading the settlers that a 'multi-racial society' is not merely a politician's cliché. But his Capricorn Society has made less impression than he hoped.

As soon as we left the main road Daphne and I found

ourselves in the same dusty, dreary country as surrounds
Serima – rough tracks, low scrub, occasional patches of
mealies and clusters of huts – we got lost; enquiries for a
Mission led us to an Anglican school where boys were
playing football; a teacher gave us a guide to the Jesuits.
They were playing football there, too, and some boys
were splashing in an iron water-tank. There were four or
five priests, in their working clothes of shirts and shorts;
two at least of them men of high scholarship. We had lost
so much time in getting there that we could barely greet
our friend before setting back. He does not repine either
for Farm Street or for Salisbury. Although they are so
near (when one knows the way) to Mirandellas, he and
his companions see few white people except the Native
Commissioner. Their life is devoted to the Mashona, at
the central school and in touring the villages. I have seen
lonelier and more comfortless missions in many parts of
the world – in British Guiana, for instance, where up
country I stayed with a solitary priest whose greeting
was: 'You are most welcome. I have been hoping for
someone to come and pull out two of my teeth' – but the
outward aspect of this station has a penetrating drabness.

What is known of Mashona history is ignominious;
they were the prey of the Matabele before white men
appeared in the country. Like the slum-dwellers of in-
dustrial England in the last century, they get very drunk
rather often. They clearly enjoy football and splashing
in the water. The missionaries say they have some
enthusiasm in religious exercises. But on the superficial
observer – or on me at any rate – they cast a gloom not

easily dispelled. It sat heavy on me as we bumped back
to the race-course, which we reached just as the last race
was run, and as we sped back on the high road home.

March 22nd. A last tourist trip, to the Matopos. These
famous hills are second only to the Eastern Highlands in
natural beauty, and they are much odder. At Leopard's
Rock there were comparisons to be made with other
scenery in other parts of the world. There is nothing I
know at all like the Matopos. They comprise some fifty
by thirty miles of bare granite and green valleys. The
district caught the particular fancy of Cecil Rhodes, and
it is here by his wish that he is buried on a spot which he
named 'the View of the World' which he designated as a
'Valhalla' for the heroes of the country. It is therefore a
region of particular sanctity to patriotic Rhodesians. Also
to the Matabele, who first chose it as a burial place for
their king, Mzilikazi, who led them here out of Zululand
in 1838. When pioneers rifled this royal cave, Rhodes had
it walled up and made formal reparation for the sacrilege
with the sacrifice of black oxen. But there are older
associations than the Matabele. The rock clefts are
covered with bushmen drawings of men, animals and
unidentified shapes, categorized by archaeologists into
periods of varying skill, from, perhaps, before the beginning of the Christian era until shortly before the arrival
of the Matabele. There is also an oracle that has spoken
for at least 500 years and still speaks. It is in the custody
of the noble families of the Kalanga tribe and it is inspired
by the mysterious spirit, the Mlimo, which the American,

Burnham, claimed to have shot. The Mlimo is much concerned with rain making and diseases of cattle, but he has wider interests. It was he who in 1895 helped foment the rising by assuring the Matabele, who took over his cultus with the country, that the white men's bullets would turn to water before striking them – a delusion which in the last hundred years has afflicted Africans in widely separate and unconnected areas; in the Soudan, for instance, and in the Southern Province of Tanganyika. The priests of the Mlimo are said to have maintained an elaborate intelligence service among the whole Bantu people as far south as the Basutos. Pilgrims came, and still come, to him from there and from Swaziland and Bechuanaland. The precise position of this African Delphi, Njelele Cave, is known to some whites but not publicly proclaimed. The official guide-book says: 'Very many Africans look upon Mlimo as a powerful and beneficent deity and upon his worship as an important institution. For that reason we have omitted any details of the location of this cave and visitors are asked to respect its privacy by not searching for it by themselves. To visit Njelele at the invitation of one of the *Abantwana bo Mlimo* is, of course, quite another matter and usually it is not difficult for anyone having the confidence of the local Kalango to receive such an invitation.'

I doubt whether many of the visitors would be particularly interested. They come to picnic, fish, catch butterflies and photograph the game. Most modern Rhodesians seem to me morbidly incurious about native customs and beliefs. Their predecessors fought the natives, stole their cattle, tricked them into making concessions, but they perforce studied them in a rough and ready way and mixed with them. Dr Jameson was sworn as a member of Lobengula's bodyguard and, in violation of his oath, led the attack against him. Selous, the most famous hunter and explorer of Rhodesia, had a black wife; a mulatto daughter of his lives in the outskirts of Salisbury today. The Afrikaan conception of 'apartheid' would have been alien and (I think) outrageous to most of the early adventurers.

I have (or rather had, for his tour of duty ended shortly after my visit) a nephew serving as A.D.C. to the Governor of Southern Rhodesia – a dignitary not to be confused with the Governor-General of the Federation. This dutiful young man arranged my trip to the Matopos with practical efficiency, coming out to fetch me and installing me for the night in great comfort at Government Lodge – the Governor's official residence in Salisbury.

Next day *March* 23rd we left at dawn and took the aeroplane to Bulawayo. A car was waiting there to take us to breakfast at Government House. This is the house built by Rhodes for his own use on the site of Lobengula's kraal. It is a charming, low, shady, building in the Dutch-colonial style. In an outbuilding there is the model of a reconstruction of the kraal as it stood in Lobengula's day, part cantonment, part cattle ranch. In the trim garden stands a surprisingly paltry tree which is pointed out as the one under which he held court. There is nothing else

at Government House or anywhere in his kingdom to
awake his memory; his grave is unknown, his treasure
stolen or lost, his posterity unrecognized. But he haunts
it yet, a deeply tragic figure from Shakespearean rather
than from classical drama; Lear, Macbeth, Richard II, he
has a touch of them all. What a part for Mr Paul Robeson
could be written of his doom. He was the victim of
history. The Matabele kingdom was a military institution
aptly organized to survive and prosper in any age before
Lobengula's. He inherited a superb army, and war was
the condition of his authority. The young warriors had
to blood their spears. If the white men had not entered
central Africa his dynasty might have lasted centuries.
He was personally brave, majestic, intelligent and honourable. The curious thing is that he genuinely liked white
men, protected them when it was in his power to annihi-
late, kept his word when he might have tricked them.
The white men he met were mostly scoundrels. It is
generally supposed that it was their avarice alone which
overthrew him. Mashonaland proved a disappointment to
the prospectors. Driven by the hope of finding another
Rand or another Kimberley, they clamoured for Matabeleland. Contemporary accounts of Lobengula's last
decade make shameful reading. The white concession
hunters camped all round him; they brought him champagne and rifles; Dr Jameson treated him with morphia;
a squadron of Life Guards paraded before him in full
dress; the Jesuits designed a coat-of-arms for his carriage
door. And all the time his regiments watched their huge,
naked monarch grow fat and muddled. He wrote person-

ally to Queen Victoria for guidance. He sent ambassadors to Cape Town who were kidnapped or murdered. And the young warriors grew mutinous.

It was not only the fortune hunters who welcomed his fall. Before attacking, Rhodes sought the sanction of the missionaries, and got it. It is hard to realize now that at the time of the Diamond Jubliee many men of goodwill and intelligence thought the Pax Victoriana a reality. The bloody little forays of the Matabele seemed to them a shocking anachronism. Even now you will find people of some goodwill and some intelligence who speak of Europeans as having 'pacified' Africa. Tribal wars and slavery were endemic before they came; no doubt they will break out again when they leave. Meantime, under European rule in the first forty years of this century there have been three long wars in Africa on a far larger scale than anything perpetrated by marauding spearmen, waged by white men against white, and a generation which has seen the Nazi régime in the heart of Europe had best stand silent when civilized and uncivilized nations are contrasted. But the missionaries genuinely believed that the autocrats, their fierce aristocracies and their witches were the only grave impediments to the establishment of the sign of charity. Fr Prestage, S. J., who gave his whole life to natives of Rhodesia, wrote: 'If ever there was a just war, the Matabele War was just.'

Lobengula's flight after defeat, aged and half stupefied; his pathetic attempts to make peace by giving a bag of sovereigns to two troopers (who stole it); his wagon of treasure – carrying what? the rubbishy gifts of his

European courtiers? ivory? gold? – driven into some cleft in the rocks, hidden, perhaps pilfered, perhaps still there; his disappearance across the river and death, it is said, by smallpox, in an unknown spot; all this comprises the very stuff of poetic drama.

After breakfast we drove back to Bulawayo. It has a quiet, old-fashioned air which, I am told, the inhabitants do not particularly relish. Not long ago it was the commercial capital of Rhodesia. Now Salisbury has cut it out. There are no skyscrapers here. The shops have a sombre, provincial respectability like those of the Scottish Lowlands. The chemist has a panelled window surmounted by the traditional glass bottles of coloured water and inside the drawers and jars with the Latin labels that used to delight one's childhood. Salisbury chemists are ablaze with advertisements of patent medicines, cosmetics and baby-foods. The tobacconist kept better cigars than I had found in Salisbury. There is a good museum, stocked with fauna below; native weapons and costumes upstairs. Until lately natives were not allowed to look at these relics of their past; now the whole place is open to them and they come in large numbers. (The prohibition had no ideological significance. It was simply that the curator's staff, whose offices were on that floor, did not want to be disturbed by chatter.) We saw the soapstone birds and shards collected at Zimbabwe, visited the mineralogist whose task it is to examine specimens of ore and gems brought in to him – he had something of particular interest that morning; was it an emerald? – visited the archaeologist who had spent the previous summer at Zimbabwe and heard from him the tentative opinion that the most impressive parts of the ruins are all of recent, Bantu construction, and then drove up into the Matopos.

Rhodes's original estate, which he left in trust to the colony, consists of 95,700 acres, the agricultural and arable part divided into fifteen farms let to tenants, and the rocky remainder, which is laid out and maintained as a pleasure ground. This is the Matopo Park, entered through gates presented by a member of the Beit family, which encloses Rhodes's grave on his View of the World. Beyond this there are some quarter of a million acres added by proclamation in 1953.

These do not come under the control of the Rhodes Trustees but of the National Parks Department, who have laid out roads, dammed streams, and generally set out to make the place attractive to white tourists. When the project was first investigated in 1946 there were found to be some 17,500 native families in occupation with 13,800 head of stock. The officials decided there was room for only 400 families and 4,000 cattle. The natives had no wish to move. Many of them had quite clear memories of Rhodes's funeral, and of Col. Rhodes's subsequent speech in which, with undisguised emotion, he had said: 'As a proof that I know the white man and the Matabele will be brothers and friends for ever, I leave my brother's grave in your hands. I charge you to hand down this sacred trust to your sons that come after you and from generation to generation and I know if you do this my brother will be pleased.'

Would the Great White Chief be pleased, they asked, to see them turned out in under fifty years to make way for picnic parties from the cities? Eventually the decision was modified; some 700 families with ten head of cattle a piece have been allowed to remain.

There is now a small, demarcated island of 'native reserve' and a large area clear of it to the south, similarly allotted. These areas enjoy the rugged, natural character of the Park from which their inhabitants are excluded. Was this what the Great White Chief and Col. Rhodes had in mind? Was this, it is perhaps not impertinent to wonder, quite what the great concourse of native mourners were saluting when at the obsequies of 10th April 1902 they broke out into cries of (I quote from the guide book) 'N'Kosi'?

One can now drive to the foot of the hill called 'the View of the World' and an easy climb takes one to the summit. The panorama is indeed stupendous and worthy of all that has been written and said of it. Rhodes in naming it did not claim it was the finest 'view' in the world; he meant rather that from this quite modest eminence one does in that clear light and unbroken horizon get, as the guide-book says, 'a strange impression of looking out over the uttermost parts of the earth'. It is a curious fact that aeroplanes have added nothing to our enjoyment of height. The human eye still receives the most intense images when the observer's feet are planted on the ground or on a building. The aeroplane belittles all it discloses.

The most prominent man-made object is the memorial

to thirty-four soldiers who were killed at the Shangani River in 1893, the advance party of the force pursuing Lobengula. It was by Rhodes's express wish and in opposition to the sentiment of many of the people round Fort Victoria that the bones were brought here from Zimbabwe, where they were first buried. They were, as the inscription simply states, 'Brave Men'; that is to say, they fought to death in circumstances when neither retreat nor surrender was possible. Their monument is a massive erection of granite over thirty feet in height, bearing their life-sized full-length portraits in bronze high-relief by John Tweed, R.A. It is in striking contrast to the other three graves on the hill which are plain slabs of granite and brass under which lie Rhodes, Jameson and at a little distance and distinguished by the gracious appeal 'R.I.P.', Sir Charles Coghlan, the first Prime Minister of Southern Rhodesia.

At Rhodes's funeral the Bishop of Mashonaland read a poem of four stanzas composed by Kipling for the occasion. The theme was Vision:

> *Dreamer devout by vision led*
> *Beyond our guess and reach,*

The terms of panegyric amount almost to apotheosis:

> *This Power that wrought on us and goes*
> *Back to the Power again.*

And:

> *There till the vision he foresaw*
> *Splendid and whole arise*
> *And unimagined Empires draw*
> *To council neath his skies,*

The immense and brooding Spirit still,
Shall quicken and control.

That was written only fifty-seven years ago and already every prediction has been belied.

In his own lifetime, and largely by his own imprudence and dishonesty, he had seen Afrikaaners and British in South Africa hopelessly embittered. Today his great project of the all-British Cape to Cairo route has lost all meaning; the personal, honourable ascendency of Great White Chiefs has degenerated into 'apartheid'. One is tempted to the trite contrast of the achievements of the politician and of the artist; the one talking about generations yet unborn, the other engrossed in the technical problems of the task at hand; the one fading into a mist of disappointment and controversy, the other leaving a few objects of permanent value that were not there before him and would not have been there but for him. But Rhodes was not a politician; or rather he was a minor one. He was a visionary and almost all he saw was hallucination.

He was not, as Jameson disastrously was, a man of action. He was neither a soldier nor an explorer. Much has been made of the incident of his going out almost alone into the Matopos to make peace with the dissident Matabele. It was a courageous act, admirably performed, but in fact it was precisely what Fr Prestage had done with another group of Matabele chiefs four months earlier. The Matabele were then hopeless and leaderless. The promised immunity to rifle fire had proved to be an illusion. They could have been a considerable nuisance if they had continued to sulk with their spears in the inaccessible hills; but they were a defeated people. The significant feature of the celebrated Indabas was the personal effect Rhodes made. He was known to the Matabele only by repute. There can be no doubt that after those meetings they looked to him with something of the awe they had accorded their kings. African politicians who are now idolized, might with profit remember how capriciously these emotions can be aroused among their people.

Rhodes was a financier. He made a huge fortune very young at a time when other huge fortunes were being made. But the Kimberley millionaires were few and they were not lucky prospectors but assiduous business men. Rhodes's predominant skill was in the market, in negotiating combinations, monopolies and loans, in beguiling shareholders, in keeping up the price of Chartered Company Stock when it never paid a dividend, in using first-hand information to buy and sell, in creating, imposing and preserving a legend of himself that calmed the stock-market. And money for him was not an end; it was not the means to pleasure or even to personal power; it was the substance of his dreams.

There is a connexion between celibacy and 'vision', both at the lowest – Hitler – and the highest – the contemplative. Rhodes inhabited a half world somewhere between. It is the childless who plan for posterity. Parents are too busy with the concerns of the moment.

There is an attractive side to Rhodes's character; his experimental farms; his taste in the houses he chose to live in; his respect for native pieties. The scholarships he founded at Oxford set a model which has been followed in other countries, whose confidence in their 'way of life' is so strong that they believe they must only be known to be loved. It is noteworthy that his scholarships were for Americans, colonials and Germans. The Latin countries were excluded. For his obsessive imagination was essentially puerile. His first Will, made before he had much to leave, provided for the foundation of a kind of secret society dedicated to the supremacy of the Anglo-Saxon race. He had a schoolboy's silly contempt for 'dagoes'; for the whole Mediterranean-Latin culture. He set out quite deliberately to provoke war with the Portuguese and was only stopped by Lord Salisbury. He saw in his fantastic visions of the future world state of English, Germans and North Americans. But his most important associates both in South Africa and in Europe were nearly all Jews. That is the point, so often missed, of Belloc's 'Verses to a Lord'. There was no conceivable reason why Jews as much as Gentiles should not make fortunes in the diamond and gold fields, or why they should not welcome an exercise of force to facilitate their business. What was absurd was Rhodes's promoting their interests with idiotic cries of Anglo-Saxon racialism.

Jameson, who lies near him, is remembered now only for his upsetting of 'the apple cart'. He was a foolish, not very scrupulous, rather engaging adventurer who first made himself popular as a doctor by maintaining the labour supply at the diamond mines by his refusal in his professional capacity to quarantine them at a time of epidemic. Lobengula particularly liked him and his morphia. He was no visionary but a faithful dog and he too was celibate.

There was something noble in his adoration of Rhodes. He took physical risks and endured hardships such as Rhodes never knew. He made no fortune. As far as is known Rhodes had no communication with him, though he was broken-hearted, from the time of his raid until his release from prison.

We left the View of the World and drove through the hills along the roads which have been admirably devised for the pleasure of sight-seers, pausing to look at clefts in the rocks covered in drawings of men and animals that have now vanished from the hills – giraffe, rhinoceros. The fauna most common there now are baboons. We saw plenty of these but none of the famous sable antelope, nor cobras, puff adders nor pythons. My nephew had provided a fine hamper. We ate our lunch beside a lake; no one else was in sight except a passing Matabele guide in smart uniform.

The afternoon aeroplane took us back to Salisbury in time for tea at Government Lodge. I had been there several times before, but never by daylight. I was able to see and admire the garden that has been the particular contribution of the Governor's wife.

March 25th. That evening John and I gave a small dinner-party, my own farewell combined with the 'coming-out' of his second daughter. At the table we were predominantly British; there was one Prussian; Rhodes would have approved of that; but there were also French, Hungarians, Greeks, the dagoes he wished to exclude from his mad Anglo-Saxon world; who now form a large and lively part of the population. The restaurant was Portuguese, newly opened at the top of one of the new tall buildings. French cooking has not yet reached Rhodesia (it is, I am told, rapidly disappearing from London), but Salisbury has now reached the degree of sophistication when restaurants go in and out of fashion. The Portuguese cooking and wine were excellent. We were far from the bottled sauces and tinned vegetables that used to encumber so many of the tables of British Africa.

March 26th. The anniversary of Cecil Rhodes's death. Public notices had been inviting the citizens to commemorate the event at his statue in the main square of the town. The Governor was there, some police and some school-children, but it was not an imposing gathering. Rhodes's picture hangs in all public places and in some private ones, but the cultus seems tepid. He is as much revered by the new generation of Salisbury as, perhaps, is Abel Janszoon Tasman in Hobart. The 'immense and brooding Spirit' no longer 'quickens and controls'.

Early that afternoon I took the aeroplane for Cape Town.

8 · Return

March 26th continued.

All airports I know are forbidding; Johannesburg, where we stopped late that afternoon, is surely the worst in the world. We were herded down into a concrete basement; a sort of bomb shelter furnished with half a dozen doors into which, one by one, we were directed. No one was seen to emerge. A lamp over the door gave the signal and a sallow young woman announced through a microphone 'Passenger Waugh will proceed to door number 3'. It was like the play of Dunsany's I once saw, in which a group of criminals were summoned to death by (I think) an oriental idol. When I reached the appointed place I found a civil enough young immigration officer who stamped my passport and released me by a further door into a passage which led to the upper level and a waiting-room of the normal kind.

The aeroplane brought me to Cape Town that night and I drove straight to the *Pendennis Castle* and slept on board in comfort.

March 27th.   Good Friday. We do not sail until evening, but I do not go ashore. It is pleasanter now to see from the decks the famous view of Table Mountain and the decent old city.

Anyone who travelled by troopship to the Middle East in the days when the Mediterranean was impassable must have grateful – some, I believe, have tender – memories of the hospitality of Cape Town. After weeks at sea with blackened portholes we found a town all alight, but much more than this we found what seemed to be the whole population extended to welcome us, the whole quay lined with cars to take us into the country. I remember the scene at night with the men returning to the ship, some drunk, some sober, all happy, laden, many of them, with great bunches of grapes like the illustrations in old Bibles of the scouts returning to the Israelites in the desert with evidence of the Land of Promise flowing with milk and honey. It is a memory I prefer to maintain intact. Few peoples anywhere, I suppose, deserve the government they get. Too many English voices are at the moment raised to reproach the South Africans for me to join in the clamour.

There was no religious observance on board. Instead the ship was thrown open to visitors who thronged it all day; ladies dressed as though for Ascot, youths dressed for goodness knows what in shorts, many of them with beards, an emblem apparently of republican sympathies.

The stewards carefully hid the ash-trays and tea-spoons from souvenir collectors.

The *Pendennis Castle* is a ship well worth visiting; she is the flagship of the line, now on her second voyage. When the sight-seers went ashore I explored her at leisure; she is spacious, ingeniously planned and brightly decorated, manned by stewards more experienced than most of the young men in *Rhodesia Castle*.

They were hard worked, for the passenger list was

completely full; quite different company from my fellow-travellers on the east coast, older and more opulent; no missionaries, no officials, no young people going to work. A cinema comedian was the only notable on board. He made himself very popular in leading the mild festivities. I was where I belonged; in the returning migration of those who had fled the English winter.

Comfortable, uneventful days succeed one another; a sense of well-being and repose after not very arduous travel. A half-day's stop at Las Palmas to refuel; a morning pottering round the streets of that charming town. Then on again punctually and smoothly.

April 10th. Southampton in the early morning; effortless disembarkation. Nothing to record except appreciation of a happy fortnight. When last I returned from Africa it was by air and I landed, like everyone else, cramped and sleepless and fit only for days of recuperation. Today I came ashore buoyantly; very different from the old fellow who crept into the train south two months ago. That was the object of the trip.

I came abroad, as I noted at the time, with the intention of eschewing 'problems' and of seeking only the diverting and the picturesque. Alas, that is not possible. 'Problems' obtrude. There was in my youth a film which opened superbly with Buster Keaton as an invalid millionaire landing from his yacht in a Central American Republic. He is enjoying a rest-cure. The people of the country are enjoying a revolution. He progresses, if I remember rightly, in a bath-chair, up the main street, totally unaware of the battle raging round him. As the dead and wounded double up before him, he raises his hat in acknowledgement of what he takes to be their bows of welcome. One cannot long travel in that way. From Algeria to Cape Town the whole African continent is afflicted by political activities which it is fatuous to ignore and as fatuous to dub complacently an 'awakening'. Men who have given their lives to the continent can do no more to predict the future than can the superficial tourist. All know that there is no solution in parliamentary democracy. But, ironically enough, the British Empire is being dissolved on the alien principles which we ourselves imported, of nineteenth-century Liberalism.

The foundations of Empire are often occasions of woe; their dismemberment, always.

The Austro-Hungarian Empire fell because the component peoples were urged to attribute their ills to thwarted nationalism. No one, I suppose, in their former dominions had a happier or better life as the result of 'self-determination', though Czechs and Croats and Magyars were enormously more civilized in 1918 than the native nations of Africa today.

I suppose the nearest historical comparison to modern Africa is the reality behind the fiction of Buster Keaton's Latin America. The Spanish monarchy was dispossessed by local revolutionaries who spoke the already antiquated language of the Enlightenment. A century of chaos and tyranny followed and is not yet everywhere abated.

The consciences of the English are unnaturally agitated by Africa. The questions that greet the returned tourist are not: 'Did you have a good time?' but: 'What about apartheid? What about Hola? What about the imprisonment of the politicians?' I can only reply: 'Don't know.'

In Tanganyika I found nothing but good-will towards the Africans darkened with grave doubts of the future. In Rhodesia there is an infection from the south of racial insanity. I heard of a Catholic woman who was offended because an itinerant priest said Mass for her on her stoep with a black server. But the story was told me as something disgusting.

I heard people of 'pioneer stock' say: '*You* can't understand. *We* remember the time when these people threatened to kill us', while at the same time cordially entertaining Germans. The more recent, more civilized immigrants have none of these unreasoning emotions. They regard the natives as a peasantry and treat them accordingly, but if their sons go to local schools they are in danger of picking up more than an unattractive accent. Every year in Rhodesia the status of the native is being slightly raised. Apartheid is the creation of the Boers. It is the spirit of equalitarianism literally cracked. Stable and fruitful societies have always been elaborately graded. The idea of a classless society is so unnatural to man that his reason, in practice, cannot bear the strain. Those Afrikaaner youths claim equality with you, gentle reader. They regard themselves as being a cut above the bushmen. So they accept one huge cleavage in the social order and fantastically choose pigmentation as the determining factor. Cardinal Garcias and the Hottentot are equal on one side; you, gentle reader, and the white oaf equal on the other; and there is no passage across that preposterous frontier.

I was witness, many years ago, to a happy product of this disordered logic, when, having run short of money in Cape Town, I travelled home third class. I embarked with some slight apprehensions, which were quite otiose. Our quarters were clean, our food abundant and palatable; there was only one privation – lack of space. We were four in a cabin and there was simply not enough room for all of us to sit on deck or in the saloon. I forget how many baths and lavatories there were, but I remember there was usually a queue. One black man travelled with us. In deference to South African susceptibilties he had a four-berth cabin to himself. More than this he had a lavatory, a bathroom and an armchair all placarded: 'For the use of non-European passengers only'. He was a man of studious disposition and he had a very comfortable voyage. I greatly envied his three week's solitude. A similar situation existed on my first visit at the University of Rhodesia, where a single black girl enjoyed quarters designed for many.

In Washington D.C., when I was last there, I visited a segregated Pets' Cemetery. The loved ones were separated not by their own colour but by that of their owners; black and white pets of white women lay indifferently in one quarter; black and white pets of black women in another.

Racialism is dotty and rather modern, but it is widespread. One is certainly not more conscious of it in Africa (except in the Union) than in America.

And acts of violence by the police are also widespread everywhere in the world. It would be interesting to know how often during the last five years the Indian police have (quite properly) opened fire on rioters and charged them with *lathis*. These incidents are not given much prominence in the English papers. It was my impression, when I was in India lately and reading the local press, that there was rioting somewhere in that huge country almost every day. No one in his senses thinks it a good thing that Kenya prison warders should kill their prisoners; but no one in his senses should think it peculiar to Kenya. Cruelty and injustice are endemic everywhere.

It is noble to expiate the sins of mankind vicariously in a hermit's cell. Failing that heroic remedy, let me gratefully accept the good things that the world still offers and do not, I beg you, try and impute guilt for things entirely outside my control.

I have had a happy two months and I won't let the weekly papers spoil them for me.